BRAIN GAMES®

BIBLE
CROSSWORD PUZZLES

Prayers, Parables & Prophets

Large Print

pil

Publications International, Ltd.

21. Not yet risen for the day
23. Dismantle sail supports
26. Horseman of yore
27. Bubbly from Catalonia
30. HE AILS (prophet anagram)
33. Nepalese climber
36. Future oak, maybe

37. Brilliant ones
38. Sound of frustration
41. Part of an inch
42. Volunteer's offer
44. Salon treatment, for short
47. Mideast land, initially
48. Corp. big shots
49. Hoped-for proposal reply

Answers on page 179.

Flowers & Plants

ACROSS

1. Priestly robe's hem three-color pattern elements (Exodus 28:33)
10. _____ Lingus (Irish carrier)
11. Has misgivings about
12. Hollywood's "Norma _____"
13. Tense tennis situation
15. The disciples were accused of eating _____ on the Sabbath (Luke 6:1–2)
16. Tire surfaces
17. At the pinnacle of
19. Overt delight
20. _____-earth metals
21. Emulate a vagabond
22. Sibelius's "Valse _____"
23. Shiny silk fabric
26. Sprinkle
28. Junior spoiler, perhaps
31. Lightly burn
32. Nigerian-born singer
34. Dakota, once: abbr.
35. Web forums ancestor
37. Cheery sounds
39. Arsenal workers
41. Big Blue corp.
42. Stable shade
43. Not a particular
44. One of the three gifts of the Magi (Matthew 2:11)

DOWN

1. Use a spyglass
2. Central American leader
3. Weaken, as confidence
4. Costume
5. 1990s cartoon dog
6. Phoenician deity
7. Recurrent themes
8. Sound receiver
9. Governing body
10. Autumn bloom
14. People "Took branches of _____, and went forth to meet him" (John 12:13)
15. Manna was compared to the seed of this culinary herb (Numbers 11:7)
18. Bakery purchase

24. Lab gel medium
25. Sporty Italian wheels
26. Arab prince (var.)
27. Respiratory illness
29. Trojan War hero
30. Excessively charming

32. Cousin of poison ivy
33. All together
36. Beach bird
38. Like a pocket dict.
40. "The Da Vinci Code" director Howard

Answers on page 180.

Jesus' Disciples

ACROSS

2. Unappetizing bowlfuls
6. Primal Scream's "Movin' ____"
9. Text digitization meth.
11. Makes a jump
13. Carpet feature
15. "Lebbaeus, whose surname was ____" (Matthew 10:3)
17. "Tarzan" extra
18. Repudiates
19. Footwear altercation
20. Reproduction's opp.
21. Easy to break
23. Make extremely upset
24. Thin strip
26. In art, his apostolic symbol is a skinning knife
31. Potential taxpayer
32. Honker
34. Aimed high
37. In the matter of
38. Mellow
39. Sailboat poles
41. Queensland bird
42. Faithful followers
44. Be follower
45. Showy success
46. Old poetic conjunction
47. Film ____
48. Purse closers

DOWN

1. Ballpark staple
2. Crushed ice drink
3. Quaint retail word
4. Carrots platemates
5. Ed.'s request, sometimes
6. WWII intelligence agency
7. Far from fitting
8. Vatican-related
10. Winged figure described in 2 Chronicles 3:11–12
12. Babyish
14. The first apostle (Matthew 10:2)
16. Enjoy archaeology
19. Sunflower stalk
21. Flaxen
22. "____ out?"

24. Bankable actor
25. Relating to the diaphragm
27. Tara in the tabloids
28. Stores, as fodder
29. Less arid
30. His brother John was also an Apostle (Matthew 4:21)
33. Gave orders

35. Apostle, _____ the Canaanite (Matthew 10:4)
36. Demoted planet
37. Abstract sculptor Jean
39. Look over cursorily
40. Bread to stuff
42. "_____ Rosenkavalier"
43. Mercedes models

Answers on page 180.

Biblical Nations

ACROSS

1. Short boxing punch
4. Crust on a wound
8. Bygone Dodge
10. Ancient Middle Easterner or a person guided by materialism
12. Chin attachment?
13. Nap
15. Russian writer Maksim
17. Long and twisty
19. Widescreen choice: abbr.
21. Aerosmith front man
22. Raguel the _____, father of Hobab (Numbers 10:29)
27. 7 a.m. staple, briefly
28. Wallet fill
29. Metric wts.
30. In-flight ETA announcer
31. Sitcom alien
32. King Arad the _____, ruler of the land promised to Israelites (Numbers 33:40)
34. Popular firewood
36. Chafe
37. Salad bar option
40. Diver's gear
44. Most chic
46. Subj. for a theologian
47. A "good" member of this group is depicted in one of the parables
48. Post-holiday store event
49. Certain doctor
50. Astrological feline

DOWN

1. Digital img. format
2. Mock phrase of insight
3. A coffin's stand
4. Glass base
5. CBS forensic series
6. Suit to _____
7. Endure
8. Freshly
9. Arithmetically competent
11. Nick of Hollywood
14. Indian antelope
16. Malay wavy dagger
18. Well-_____

20. "My Way" lyricist Paul
22. Inhabitants of the old Levantine kingdom with its capital in Dibon
23. Bay or bight
24. Vanquish
25. Car starter: abbr.
26. Autocrat
30. Biz network
32. Porcelain
33. Texas capital
35. Finalize
38. Intentions
39. Least-varying tide
41. Russian range or river
42. Nota _____
43. Adding to that
45. _____ Lanka

Answers on page 180.

The Prophet Ezekiel

ACROSS

2. Ability to communicate audibly with other people
7. Footnote abbr.
11. Nagging pain
13. Sorority character
14. Toon explorer
15. Deposited
16. The Lord did this to Ezekiel's power of 2-Across (Ezekiel 3:26)
17. McDormand on screen
19. Airport abbr.
20. Album unit
21. Unsubstantial image
25. Arrange
28. God addressed him by the title "_____ of man"
29. Ezekiel saw them in his first vision (Ezekiel 1:5–6)
33. _____ rating system
34. Herbal beverage
35. Aromatic root
39. Loud clamor
40. 365/366 dias
41. Pincered bugs
44. One of the words that was written on the scroll God ordered Ezekiel to eat (Ezekiel 2:10)
47. Paul Simon's "_____ Rock"
48. Van front?
49. Aviary sound
50. Apartment in London
51. Additionally
52. There are two in the name of his parable (Ezekiel 17)

DOWN

1. Latte option
2. Spa offering
3. Philly campus
4. Art Deco pioneer
5. Made a selection
6. Bally follower
7. Apple-cider gal
8. Cylindrical carpentry pin
9. Muse of bards
10. Ancient Mexican
12. Opera great Enrico
18. Go round
22. Peace-hand connection

23. Weak-minded
24. Burdensome duty
26. Sources of gold, e.g.
27. High-tech suffix
30. Some tires
31. Cryptic mystery
32. Physically aware
35. Type of ray
36. Tuna-can phrase

37. Verbs' mates
38. Columbus's birthplace
42. Bursting with excitement
43. Family member God told him not to grieve (Ezekiel 24:16–18)
45. 2016 Summer Olympics site
46. _____ cap

Answers on page 180.

"M" Places in the Bible

ACROSS

1. The place where Jacob had the vision of angels (Genesis 32:1–2)
8. Half a sch. year
11. Fenny tract
12. Poster color
15. Andrea _____ (sunken liner)
16. Wood finish
17. Give the gun back
19. Pembroke _____ Corgi
20. Sound on a dairy farm
21. Circular window
23. Classic
25. Perfume giant
26. Loud hit sound
28. Off base, in a way
31. Copy
32. Land where Moses dwelt (Exodus 2:15)
34. Bit of Morse code
35. Give one's two cents
37. Bovine feature
40. Chicken choice
43. Greek column
44. One way to succeed
45. Bygone British gun
46. Nova Scotia hrs
47. City near which five kings hid in a cave (Joshua 10:17)

DOWN

2. Lovingly, on sheet music
3. Let
4. Dramatic solo at the Met
5. Almost
6. A bird or a plane preceder
7. Expression of disinterest
8. Auctions off, perhaps
9. Units of geologic time
10. Here were laid the bodies of Abraham and Sarah (Genesis 23:19; 25:9)
13. Cry feebly
14. Of lung membranes
18. Ruth's country (Ruth 1:4)
20. Land in one of Paul's visions (Acts 16:9)
22. Bow of the silents

24. Injection selection
27. Restaurant handout
29. Broadened
30. Relative of a flute
32. Superior power
33. Forest grazers

36. Groan inducers
38. Part of the spine
39. Be fond of
41. Filmmaker Burton
42. Depot, for short

Answers on page 181.

Old Testament Prayers

ACROSS

1. Core
4. Something done ineptly
9. Comparatively twisted
11. Art, nowadays
12. Place where Elijah prayed to the Lord to send fire and burn the offering (1 Kings 18:36–38)
15. Held dear
17. Early programming language
18. Covenant
19. Plant anew
21. _____ whim
22. Enlistees, briefly
23. Rules, informally
26. What Daniel requested from God regarding the king's dream (Daniel 2:19–23)
30. Even-speak connection
31. "The X-Files" subjects
32. Game roller
34. "Ghosts" playwright
35. Cal. heading
36. Dress cut
39. Diffuse through membrane
41. In his prayer he asked for wisdom to better govern the people of Israel (2 Chronicles 1:6–12)
44. Patriots' grp.
45. Contest-judging group
46. Change again
47. Actor Hawke

DOWN

1. Large African stork
2. It can be drawn
3. Proven
4. Fired (up)
5. Ballistic path
6. Door feature
7. Black & white treat
8. Part of the great fish out of which Jonah was praying (Jonah 2:1)
10. Short-tailed lemurs
12. Single-celled organisms
13. Autumn droppings
14. Did galley work

16. Prima _____
20. Beautician Lauder
22. Crested waterfowl
24. He prayed for the deliverance of the Israelites from the Midianites (Judges 6:13–14)
25. Uses shears
27. "Dallas" family
28. When gunslingers dueled
29. Enjoy payback
33. Senegal's capital
35. Migrating sea trout
37. What Hezekiah pleaded with God to extend (Isaiah 38:2–5)
38. Highlander of old
40. Captain Hook's henchman
42. On the facing pg.
43. Brutus's lang.

Answers on page 181.

Bible Name Changes

ACROSS

1. Bird with long legs
5. Small partnership
8. Snail mail bringers: abbr.
12. Ambassador's asset
13. Shadrach's original name (Daniel 1:7)
14. Milk's favorite cookie
15. Rating system in chess
16. "And so on" word
17. East German currency, once
19. Takeout food request
20. Laundry action
21. Very deep places (var.)
23. Fox of "Transformers"
27. West in old movies
28. Port-au-Prince's land
30. Classified ad letters
31. Bygone Chevy van
33. Stuck around
35. Crop-killing salts
37. Nobelist Curie
40. Strident
43. Composer's work
44. Twistedly funny
45. Fresh way to start
46. New name for Solomon (2 Samuel 12:24–25)
47. Advantageous position
48. Team on a field
49. Brief "I think"
50. Large city of France

DOWN

1. "Am _____ strict?"
2. How was Joseph Justus called (Acts 1:23)
3. Rapper turned TV cop
4. Beats decisively
5. Former PM _____ May
6. Ambles
7. Yoko of Beatle history
8. Detach, as oxen
9. Old Thailand
10. Bruise preventers
11. Deep carpet
18. Opening in clothing
19. Neighbor of South Africa
21. Docs grp.

22. Nonetheless

24. The Lord

25. New name for Azariah (Daniel 1:7)

26. Discreet approval

29. Hunt holler

32. Cereal fruit

34. New name for Jacob (Genesis 32:28)

36. Abraham's original name (Genesis 17:5)

37. Lucky charm

38. Summit

39. Not polite

41. Nickname of Dr. Jones

42. Stefani of music

44. Nintendo game system

Answers on page 181.

Prayers of Jesus

ACROSS

1. Name of dead man + place where Jesus brought him back to life (John 11:38–44)
10. What could not pass away from Jesus and what he had to drink from (Matthew 26:39–42)
11. Foldable quarters
12. Mauna follower
13. Freezer forerunner
15. Dimwit
16. May celebrants
17. Ammonia derivatives
19. Alternatively
20. "Friends" friend
21. Rabbit species (var.)
23. Popular cryptocurrency
25. Ristorante dumplings
28. Mold anew
30. Singing Collins
33. Major vein
34. Beaufort-scale level
36. Roman emperor
38. Util. payment
39. Westlife's "If _____ You Go"
40. Helped
43. Great Basin St.
44. Bloodhound's asset
45. Light-switch positions
46. Whom Jesus asked his Father to forgive, while dying on the cross (Luke 23:34)

DOWN

1. French director Besson
2. Sci-fi figures
3. Molecular matter
4. Show thriftiness
5. Young_____ (tykes)
6. Fat-derived
7. Ballerina Alicia
8. Mouse cousin
9. Avoids the diner
10. Municipality-related
14. Entity that descended upon Jesus while he was praying during his baptism (Luke 3:21–22)

15. Jesus asked the Father to protect them from the evil one (John 17:6–19)

18. Closet concern

22. Two halved

23. Letters at the end of dates preceding Jesus' birth

24. "_____ were you…"

26. Zero, slangily

27. Having an effect

28. Lake Michigan port

29. Blouse part

31. Swagger

32. Most famous prayer in the Bible

34. White base for canvases

35. Bizarre

37. TV host Trebek

41. Syllable before disant

42. Duo of sinners?

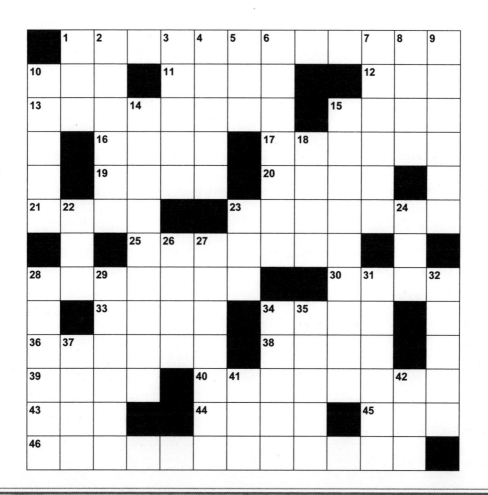

Answers on page 181.

Old Testament Anagrams

ACROSS

1. Book written by prophet Jeremiah (anagram of NOMINAL TASTE)
10. Lang. heard in Rome
11. Deepest
13. Unforeseen hang-up
14. Foretells
15. Hair slickener
17. Home in a cave
18. Book between Judges and 1 Samuel (anagram of HURT)
20. East _____ (Asian country)
23. _____ jokes
26. Baby's bed
28. Big org. come April
29. Fifth Old Testament book (anagram of MENTORED YOU)
31. Take-away matchsticks game
32. Actress Headey
33. Outside, in combinations
35. Exit line
38. Book following the Chronicles (anagram of RAZE)
40. Wrestling's _____ Flair
42. Shoelace holder
45. Sci-fi villains, often
48. Clinton's VP
49. Slanted
50. "_____ ain't broke . . ."
51. Book following Proverbs (anagram of ACCESS ELITES)

DOWN

1. Spoke like Daffy
2. Words with time or cost
3. Gentlewoman kin
4. Knighted British composer
5. Made, as a knot
6. Picture within another
7. Middle Easterner
8. Yule recipe
9. Opposite of NNW
12. Winter Palace occupants
14. Wide-ranging seabird

16. Heat conduit
19. New ID badge recipient
21. Nonspeaking performer
22. Big African antelope
24. Take _____ view of
25. Salesman's model
27. Monks from East Asia (archaic)
30. Hardly any, old-style
31. _____ novi ("Nothing about us without us")
34. Some Mozart works
36. Capital of Cameroon
37. Cuban Castro
39. Patronage
41. Sign away
43. Home for some artists
44. Big name in canals
46. Called when single
47. Floor cleaner, briefly

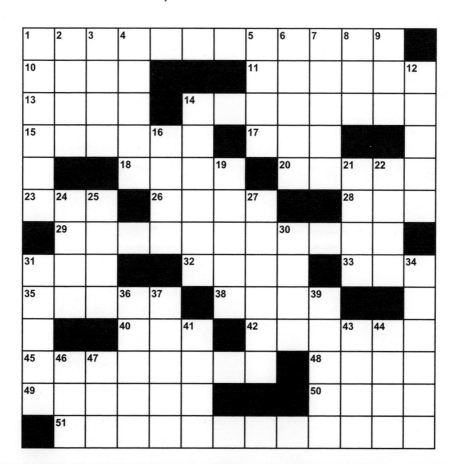

Answers on page 182.

Name the Prophet

ACROSS

2. Melodious passage
7. A governor's annual speech: abbr.
11. "Horrors!"
12. The mysteries of providence were the main theme of his book
13. Survey choice
15. 2017 hurricane
16. 60s war zone, for short
18. Kazakhstan's _____ Sea
19. Were, biblically
20. Nonchalant syllables
22. He wrote that apostasy from God is spiritual adultery
24. Occupy space
28. Gran finale?
29. Spy for the tribe of Judah
30. A tentative taste
31. Distance across
33. Academic hurdles
34. Snake, at times
38. Part of ACLU
41. Metric trillion
42. Common pluralizer
44. Nuts or bananas
45. Beehive Stater
47. Prophet that lived in Antioch and was mentioned in Acts 13:1
48. Like all thematic people of this puzzle
49. Hardly baggy
50. Ranked, in tennis

DOWN

1. One of the Gospelists
2. Boombox button
3. Bread request
4. Maureen of "Rio Grande"
5. Tossed dish
6. Division signs
7. Winter Olympics accessory
8. Cajun staple
9. Dyspepsia reliever
10. Fun 32-card game
14. His book is the last one in the Old Testament
17. Mayo cousin

21. This prophetess was also a judge
22. Reporter's question
23. Cheerless
25. Metaphor phrase
26. Paul's chosen companion in the journey through Syria and Cilicia (Acts 15:40)
27. Scout gps.
32. Huge turnout
35. Theater litter
36. Bristly hairs
37. Clean off
38. Mass vestments
39. Bewail
40. Shade of beige
42. Children's author Blyton
43. Ignored the limit
46. Deeply impress

Answers on page 182.

Bible Sayings

ACROSS

1. To do things that seem impossible (Matthew 17:20)
11. "_____ believe in yesterday"
12. Common odds ending
13. Flying irritant
14. Water boa
17. Discern from a distance
18. _____ system
19. Decorator's subtlety
21. The symbol of worship of material goods (Exodus 32:2–4)
24. Confront boldly
27. Salon worker
28. _____-friendly (green)
29. Expand upon
31. Michele on Broadway
32. "Your body is the _____ of the Holy Ghost which is in you" (1 Corinthians 6:19)
34. CEO's helper
35. A vast end-of-the-world conflict (Revelation 16:16)

37. Corp. rushing letters
38. Droops, as flowers
42. There are two in 20
44. Pay painfully
47. Supporting role
48. "_____, drink, and be merry" (Luke 12:19)
49. _____ break
50. Selfless one helping those in need (Luke 10:30–37)

DOWN

1. Extinct birds
2. "This looks bad"
3. Little fluid holder
4. Ball chaser?
5. "Tristan _____ Isolde"
6. Most spiffy
7. Service business
8. Sets up for use
9. Quick rest
10. Muddy barnyard enclosure
15. Actor Nic
16. Andean gold
20. Fascinated with

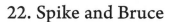

22. Spike and Bruce
23. Campus cohort
24. Greek diner staple
25. Strong server
26. Shock troop unit
29. Kelp bit
30. Far out from the coast
33. Didn't participate
34. Indigo source

36. One of the "unclean" birds (Leviticus 11:17)
39. Burglar's haul
40. Marine predator
41. Comic legend Lee
42. Price revealer
43. Kids' song ending
45. Lunch meat
46. Incoming-plane stat

Answers on page 182.

King David

ACROSS

1. Foreign dignitary: abbr.
4. Crush
8. Inland sea of central Asia
10. Length of David's reign (2 Samuel 5:4)
12. Pol follower?
13. Rues
15. Partial statues
17. Choose to participate
18. Chooses to order
20. Disney's mermaid
22. "To make ____ over all Israel" (1 Chronicles 12:38)
27. ____ dolorosa
28. Nike rival
29. Hoo preceder
30. Halliwell of pop music
31. Obstacle
32. City of David (2 Samuel 5:6–9)
34. Half of a record
36. Canceling word
37. Stop holding sack
40. Egg-white whipper
44. Regular oval shape
46. Canadian assent
47. David took them out of the brook (1 Samuel 17:40)
48. Stride
49. Yodeling feedback
50. Harris and others

DOWN

1. It may be thrown
2. ____ cross
3. Fictional rabbit
4. Untold
5. Pirate's yes
6. Mariposa lily variety
7. Musical instrument (1 Samuel 16:16–18)
8. Dormant no longer
9. Assert ownership of (with "to")
11. Label differently
14. Blub revoltingly
16. LaBeouf of "Honey Boy"
19. Island or terrier

21. Ireland, poetically
22. Superficial experiment
23. Gardner namesakes
24. Masculine
25. Super ending?
26. Part of speech
30. Goliath's residence (1 Samuel 17:4)
32. "Hero" martial artist

33. Site of a 1976 anti-Apartheid uprising
35. Dutch glazed ware
38. Provide flexibility
39. Oil cartel, for short
41. 19-Down of the screen
42. Taken to court
43. Hug go-with
45. Library cautionary sound

Answers on page 182.

Fill-in-the-Blank

ACROSS

1. "Call unto me, and I _____ thee" (Jeremiah 33:3)
11. After the fact
12. Basra resident
15. Like satellite's path
16. Graybeard
17. Twins, sometimes
18. Ocean abbr.
19. Webmaster's code
20. "_____ them that curse you" (Luke 6:28)
22. Middle of the de-n?
23. Doughnut filler
26. Plaza Hotel sprite
28. "He will regard the prayer of the _____" (Psalm 102:17)
30. Certain salt
32. Russian writer Maxim
33. Elapse quickly
34. Social slights
37. Understood, daddy-o
39. _____-Blo (fuse type)
40. Clique
43. Volcanic formation
44. Hardly deep-sea
46. Tech sch. grad
47. Pasta dish
48. "I will therefore that men pray _____, lifting up holy hands, without wrath and doubting" (1 Timothy 2:8)

DOWN

2. Am-early connector
3. Forsaken, poetically
4. High throws
5. Baba who outwitted thieves
6. From one's earliest days
7. Tennessee, for one
8. Firmly established
9. Reaction to poison ivy
10. Substances beneath the volcanoes
13. Less maintained
14. "Whatsoever ye shall ask in prayer, _____, ye shall receive" (Matthew 21:22)

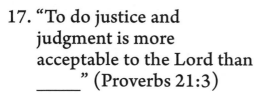

17. "To do justice and judgment is more acceptable to the Lord than _____" (Proverbs 21:3)

20. Top scores

21. Garden crawlers

24. Aswirl

25. Latin confession starter

27. Great Plains native

29. Able to be stretched

31. Much-told joke

35. Radial counterpart

36. Ironhanded

38. "Arbitrage" actor Richard

40. Dutch master, Vincent van _____

41. 18th-century composer Thomas

42. Close in distance

45. Bit of a bray

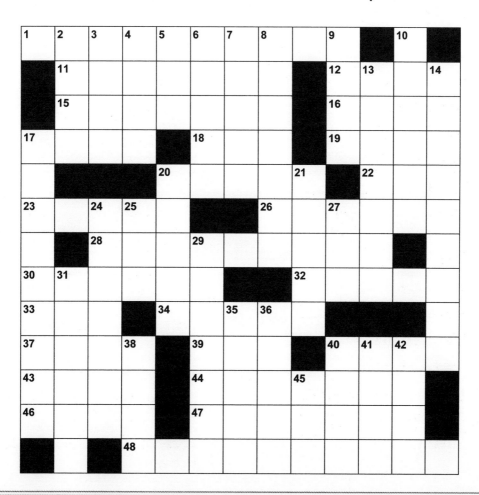

 Answers on page 183.

Words of Jesus

ACROSS

1. "I and _____ are one" (John 10:30)
7. "Suitable for all ages" rating
10. Cookware company
11. Big name in chips
13. 2016 Olympics city
14. Insertion mark
16. Llama relation
18. Made the way for
20. Was rude to
21. State north of Ill.
22. Informal alliance
24. "Whatsoever ye shall bind _____ shall be bound in heaven" (Matthew 18:18)
26. Like clarinet music
27. Profoundly deep sleep
30. Hindrance to progress
32. Mosaic square
35. One part of an equation: abbr.
36. Like some wallpapers
38. Boxing need
40. Bets
42. Exceptionless
44. Electrician's unit
45. Investigator, slangily
46. DC figure, briefly
47. Not rainy
48. "I am the way, _____, and the life" (John 14:6)

DOWN

1. Soft shoe, abbr.
2. Expect in the future
3. Cancelled
4. Unsteady
5. SAT subj.
6. Utilize again
7. Find the origin of
8. Sermon subject
9. "Let your light so shine before men, that they may see your _____" (Matthew 5:16)
12. James of "The Godfather"
15. Dress with a flare
17. Wacko
19. Prov. of Canada

21. "Man shall not live by bread alone, but by every ____" (Luke 4:4)
23. The ones yonder
25. Qualifying word
27. Most passé
28. Aspiring climber
29. Orangy tone
31. Piece of work

32. Designer Hilfiger
33. "Ye are the ____ of the earth" (Matthew 5:13)
34. Dangerous driving weather
37. Vaudeville actor Bert
39. Mind-matter link
41. Education org.
43. Folksy approval

Answers on page 183.

Old Testament Prophets

ACROSS

1. Seer who counseled King David (1 Chronicles 21:9)
4. Prepared for shipping
10. Measured lengthwise
11. Louisiana music genre
12. Act as lookout
13. Cousins of giraffes
15. Parcel, with "out"
16. St. John's bread
17. Hot dog topping
19. Jared of Hollywood
22. Sharply dressed
25. _____ expertise
27. Musical nonsense syllable
28. Flame lovers
30. Oversharing acronym
31. Hotel alternative
33. Ming antiquities
35. Fiesta morsel
36. Clearly stunned
39. Wave preceder
41. German numeral
44. Mackerel family member
45. Very small quantity
46. C.S. Lewis fantasy realm
47. One of the nine true prophetesses
48. Respiratory illness
49. Lang. course

DOWN

1. Contemptuous comment
2. Caught in _____
3. Get a hint of
4. Sources of saffron
5. Prophet who encouraged King Asa to put away the abominable idols out of the land of Judah (2 Chronicles 15:1–8)
6. Keystroke error
7. Palatable
8. Pot's front?
9. It has 66 chapters and tells us that the seraph had three pairs of wings
10. One of the five works by four major prophets
14. Carrier to Seoul
18. Church choir song
20. Munches on

21. Big volume
23. "Nessun dorma," e.g.
24. Field cover
26. Initials on invitations
29. In the single chapter he wrote there is his vision concerning Edom
32. Nightsticks

34. Old Roman magistrate
37. Gun, in slang
38. Hawaiian salutation
40. Still fighting
42. Concrete reinforcers
43. List wrap-up
44. Car-grille protector

Answers on page 183.

Biblical Kings

ACROSS

1. Not so awesome
5. Sea near Crimea
9. Hatch back?
10. Conn. summer hours
12. Tyler of "Armageddon"
14. Request earnestly
16. Robotic companion
17. One of the major kings after 38-Across (2 Chronicles 20:35)
18. "Braveheart" star Gibson
19. Smart _____
21. Frog-in-the-throat sound
24. Contemporary Persia
27. "Or _____ thought"
28. New U.S. arrivals class
29. Giant slayer and Israel's greatest king
30. Gershwin of note
31. Titter sound
32. Bygone map letters
33. Egyptian key of life
34. Frequent splashdown site
36. Kind of score
38. Wise ruler
43. Tosca or Turandot
44. Barrenness
45. Pump abbr. of old
46. Hagen of Broadway
47. Road no.
48. Walrus relative
49. Haughty type

DOWN

1. Actor Cobb
2. Danish furniture designer Jacobsen
3. Folklore
4. Brooklyn Dodgers great
5. _____ boy
6. Rookie, years later
7. Spreading fast online
8. The last king of Judah
11. Showy flowers
13. Gives a seat
15. One-sided win
20. Type of board
21. Bad monarch who was a son of 38-Across

22. Words after just or wait
23. Less lumbering
25. Camping sights
26. Travel depot
29. Loose material for packing cargo
33. Yank with 25 grand slams

35. Buenos _____
37. What a crook might go by
39. King anointed by Samuel
40. Surrealist from Barcelona
41. German male name
42. Russian veto

Answers on page 183.

The Last Supper

ACROSS

1. Part of the Bible
10. Celestial explosion
11. Nary a soul
12. Popular bug reporting software
13. Easy paces
16. Turkey feather
18. Housecat's perch
19. Pah lead-in
20. Bog flora
22. "_____ complicated"
25. Led directly to the arrest of Jesus (Luke 22:48–54)
28. Squeezing reptile
29. "For _____ of the [1-Across], which is shed for many for the remission of sins." (Matthew 26:28)
31. Dubai's fed.
32. Actress Rogers
33. Fabric amts., often
34. Any of four turtle toons
37. Debussy's "La _____"
39. Zero
41. Joined in secret
45. Least reputable
48. Conn of "Grease"
49. "Li'l" guy
50. Hosp. readings
51. "Jesus took bread, and blessed it, and brake it, and gave it to the disciples, and said, Take, eat; _____" (Matthew 26:26)

DOWN

1. Novelist Ephron
2. Emergency rescue, briefly
3. Super silly
4. State of a species being native to a single location
5. _____ Canals
6. Raiments
7. Demonstrators, often
8. First name in cosmetics
9. Fruit with a kernel
10. Imprecise ordinal
14. Male former pupil
15. Successors' places
17. "The Avengers" role
21. Saintly

22. Player with a store
23. Like some tea
24. Burnt shade
26. Helpful comparator for IT services: abbr.
27. Congruity
30. Jessica of "The Sinner"
35. He was paid 30 pieces of silver for his betrayal (Matthew 26:14–16)

36. Accused's story
38. Event in a ring
40. Camera's eye
42. Patchy
43. Feeling anxious
44. Criticize
46. Contemptuous laugh
47. Theologian's sch.

Answers on page 184.

The Persistent Widow

ACROSS

1. Kick-storm connector
4. Person the widow wanted the 1-Down to 21-Down her of (Luke 18:3)
10. Agile
12. Facto preceder
13. Collections of goods for sale
15. Confusing query
17. Altar creation
18. Bring forth
20. What she did to the 1-Down by 48-Across coming
22. Unexpected trouble
24. Explosive compounds, briefly
27. Long-running quarrel
28. Biden in the Oval Office
29. End of a cannon?
30. Inverted
33. Like champion racehorses
34. Movie star Laura
35. Basic ideas
37. Pale in the face
39. Provoked
42. _____ on (prodded)
44. Athlete's place
46. Gardener's buy
47. Madre or Mist lead-in
48. Indefinitely in time and with no interruption
49. _____ Center (LA skyscraper)

DOWN

1. The widow came to him with the same plea each time
2. Type of meson
3. Both, for openers
4. How she was living after the death of her husband
5. LAPD title
6. Clothing mishaps
7. Marital partner
8. Yes-man, e.g.
9. Future lobster
11. Squanders, as a lead
14. Stable father

16. The 1-Down "feared not God, neither _____" (Luke 18:2)
19. Clerical assemblies
21. Exact satisfaction for a wrong by punishing the one responsible
23. Fit to conclusion
25. Casual rejection
26. Four-sided figure
31. Give the boot
32. One, in Weimar
33. Back of a hit single
36. Down in points
38. Port on many laptops
40. Bit of Turkish cash
41. Multi-country money
43. Luminesce, in ad-speak
45. ID checker

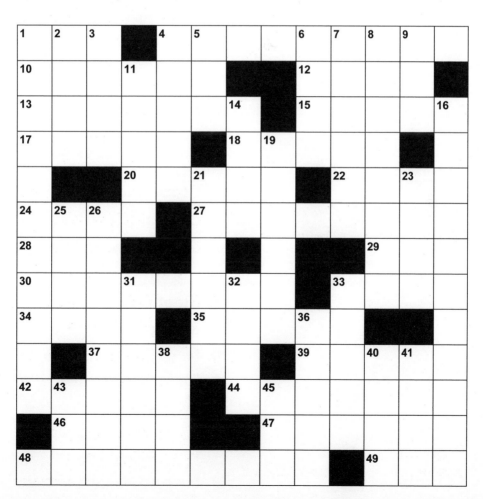

Answers on page 184.

Paul's Travels

ACROSS

1. One of Paul's destinations which gave name to 2 letters of New Testament
11. Dwarf in "The Hobbit"
12. Evans of jazz
13. Champion gymnast Korbut
14. Fide preceder
15. Tax fraud investigator
17. Bit of science?
18. Sharing maternal lines
20. Place where Paul stayed longer and performed many miracles (Acts 19)
22. Beats by a hair
25. Certain keyboard keys
26. "Can _____ honest with you?"
28. Had yearnings
30. Bobsled challenges
32. Future bloom
33. "_____ that strange?"
36. Vena _____
37. Begging place of Paul's second mission (Acts 15:22)
38. Tremble
41. Dialogue unit
44. Losing purposely
46. "May It Be" singer
47. Baseball's Berra
48. Forester's tool
49. Alternatives to Macs
50. Barjesus was one (Acts 13:6)

DOWN

2. Owl's remark
3. Cubesmith Rubik
4. _____ cat
5. Crime novelist Christie
6. Lucy of "Charlie's Angels"
7. Guinness superlative
8. Corinthian vowels
9. Blood flow stoppage
10. Kind of culture
14. Paul's companion during the first missionary journey
16. Not currently free
19. City where Paul was imprisoned (Acts 25)
21. Nicholas Gage memoir

23. Hosp. section
24. Master's follower
26. "Patience _____ virtue"
27. Drink, informally
29. Supped
31. Drag (var.)
34. Tiny grooves

35. Pitchman
37. Be of value
39. Equine foot
40. TV's Swenson
42. Proceed cautiously
43. 11 Wall St. occupant
45. Abbr. on a credit card

Answers on page 184.

Psalm 23

ACROSS

1. "Thy rod and thy staff they _____ me" (Psalm 23:4)
7. "Goodness and mercy shall follow me all the days of my _____" (Psalm 23:6)
11. Valley of grapes
12. Vowel-sequence start
13. Score in tennis
14. Passage in Latin
15. "The Lord is my _____" (Psalm 23:1)
16. Choral work
18. Tempe sch.
19. Min. collections
20. Fine lightweight cloth
24. Constructs
27. Fleur-de-_____
28. "Though I walk through the valley of the _____" (Psalm 23:4)
32. Cellular "messenger"
33. Ornamental shrub
34. Pretend to sing
38. Wetness on a lawn
39. Docs' gp.
40. Rodent-catching cats
43. "He maketh me to lie down in green _____" (Psalm 23:2)
46. Noun-forming suffix
47. Brought to maturity
48. Cry of pain
49. GPS readings
50. Chaotic situations
51. "A table before me in the presence of mine _____" (Psalm 23:5)

DOWN

1. Stuffy complaint
2. International waters
3. Wal follower
4. Type of oven
5. Place for physical therapy
6. Overtime necessitator
7. _____-di-dah
8. Food for thought
9. Unprecedented event
10. Invest with
11. Recesses
17. Caesar colleague

21. _____-Romeo
22. Factoid
23. An understanding phrase
25. USN officers
26. Seventh-day carol bird
29. Slightly firm, as pasta
30. Canonical hours
31. Anchor-chain openings

34. Capital near Titicaca
35. Pupa graduate
36. Toyota of the 1990s
37. Uncle of Oedipus
41. "Even _____ speak"
42. Bond girl Hatcher
44. Stats on some backs
45. High-fiber type of bread

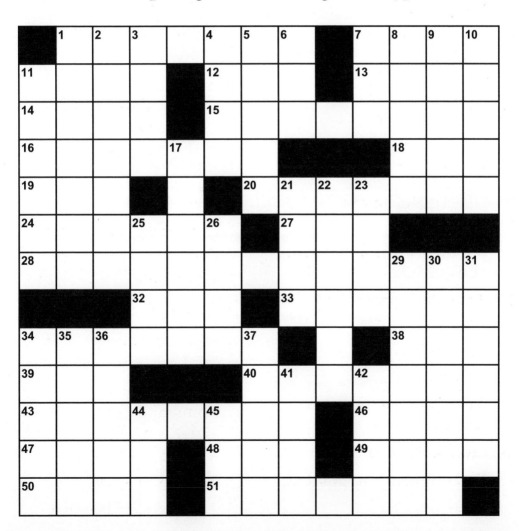

Answers on page 184.

The Prodigal Son

ACROSS

1. What the 46-Across was to his father after he returned home (Luke 15:32)
10. Monogram ltrs.
11. Appointer
14. April bloom
15. Breakfast fare
16. Make healthy
17. Certain twisted fiber
19. Accepts visitors
21. Compass dir.
22. Cal. dozen
23. Overwhelm aurally
25. What the hired 37-Across put on the 46-Across' hand (Luke 15:22)
26. Triangle descriptor
28. $20s dispensers
31. National god of the biblical Ammonites
33. Abbr. for some Spanish teachers
34. Lucy with roles
35. Trees used in shipbuilding

37. Who brought forth the fatted calf and best robe for the 46-Across (Luke 15:22–23)
40. Balladeer Burl
41. Lest
42. Authority
44. Olfactory perceptions
45. Capsize
46. The one who took his journey into a far country (Luke 15:13)

DOWN

2. Animated
3. Acclimated
4. Nastiness
5. UFO crew
6. Deadly vipers
7. Absurd
8. Without any
9. Violate the parent's commandment, what the older son never did (Luke 15:29)
12. Marlins' habitat?
13. Houston has-been co.

15. Pouring aid

16. "When he was yet a great way off, his father saw him, and had _____" (Luke 15:20)

18. Speed away

20. Anatomical enclosure

24. A mighty one struck the land where the 46-Across went and wasted his substance (Luke 15:14)

25. Pass target

27. Commandment word

29. Current thing

30. Explorer Polo

32. Refuges

34. Catch cowboy-style

36. Japanese fencing

38. Diversify

39. Cockily confident

43. Big swinger

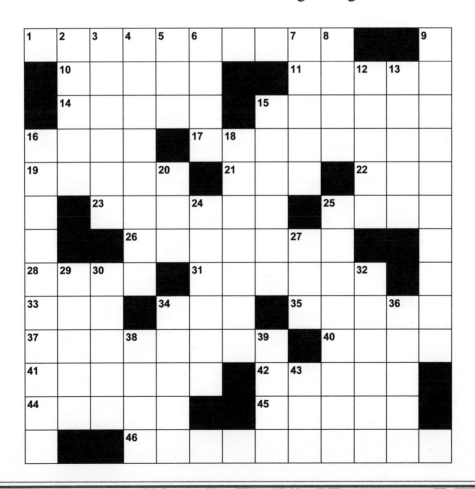

Answers on page 185.

New Testament Anagrams

ACROSS

1. Steamed bun
4. College supporters, often
9. Asian restaurant general
12. Exhibit fallibility
13. Cuban coins
14. Field-of-study suffix
15. New Testament book (anagram of LAST AGAIN)
17. Burnt-crisp link
18. Hits send
19. State of panic
20. Zesty
21. Kazakh waters
23. The comical Caesar
24. Quitter's cry
25. Two-part New Testament book (anagram of TARNISH ICON)
30. Chilean peaks
31. Take in a little food
33. Scary African flies
36. "_____ been tricked!"
38. New Testament book (anagram of CATS)
39. Brothers of bankruptcy
40. _____-Jongg
41. New Testament book (anagram of PINE ASHES)
43. _____-existing conditions
44. Evaluate
45. Away from SSW
46. Old gridiron gp.
47. Greek wraps
48. Cent start?

DOWN

1. Fathers, biblically
2. Language spoken by Jesus
3. Actor Bloom
4. Well
5. Flowery rings
6. NATO member
7. Queens and kings
8. Fizzling sound
9. Pastoral epistle of the New Testament (anagram of TUTSI)
10. Tea-time treat
11. Tennis pro Naomi
16. Corp. bailed out in 2008

19. Pest hopping on hounds
21. Initial chips
22. _____ Baba
24. Give too little money
26. Subjects of many tests
27. Showbiz connections
28. Mathematician John Von _____
29. African plain

32. Some are not perfect
33. City on a bay
34. Winter wear
35. Merman in old musicals
36. Positive responses
37. "_____ get it now!"
39. Toy block maker
41. Chick of the future
42. "Ben-_____"

Answers on page 185.

The Prophetess Deborah

ACROSS

1. Aromatherapy facility
4. Height, in combinations
8. "How hard can _____?"
12. "_____ in Israel," self-describing words of Deborah (Judges 5:7)
13. Contract sealer: abbr.
14. Climactic start?
15. Sorrowful sort
16. Some bruise easily
18. Compound in detonators
20. Relating to the eye
22. Biblical land: abbr.
24. Service abbr.
25. Speedy ski run
27. Deborah and Barak's song genre (Judges 5:2–31)
29. Finger-pointers
30. Small drink
32. Very tall mountain
33. Guided the car
36. Noted current
39. Gentlewoman
40. "It comes _____ surprise"
42. Freeze
44. Old record label
45. Deborah was known as a prophetess and a _____ (Judges 4:4)
46. Estimator's words
47. Hockey missile
48. 2021 "_____ All That"

DOWN

1. Part of Deborah's song refers to his death (Judges 5:24–27)
2. Baseball great Satchel
3. Jargon
4. Implied part of ESL
5. Mexican coins
6. Fierce badger of India
7. Leave off
8. Humble response
9. Soft silvery metal
10. Small stinger
11. Faults
17. From then till now
19. Singer Lionel

21. Mineral harvested from dry lake bed
23. Certain ID
25. Relating to heartbeat rates
26. Played up big
27. Kilmer of Hollywood
28. Looms
29. Many New Mexicans
31. Core values
33. Real mix-up
34. Deborah dwelt between _____ and Bethel (Judges 4:5)
35. Introductions handler
37. Company emblem
38. Chain to buy some stacks
41. Big finish?
43. Brief reproach

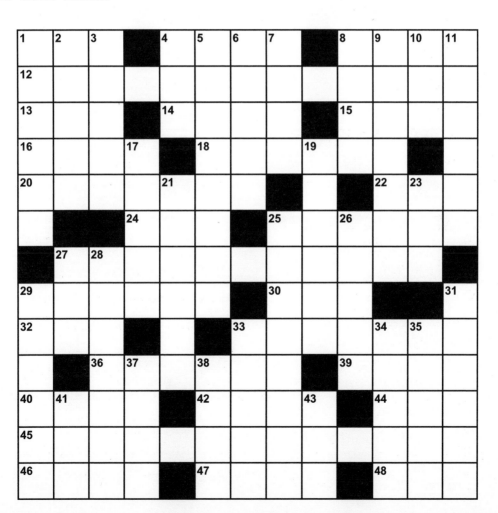

Answers on page 185.

Joseph

ACROSS

1. Give a casual greeting
5. Export-import duties
11. Vow on a stand
12. Scotsman
14. Poor, chance-wise
15. Relatively unimportant
17. Lecture locale
18. Particle theory
20. "Voice of Israel" author
23. Supermodel Klum
26. Cape Town currency
27. Lawyer, by trade
29. Went by paddleboat
31. Sign up for the service
33. Bobbing on water
34. "Survivor" setting, often
35. Part of a comic strip
37. Legendary hammer-wielder
38. Columbus, by birth
42. Insubstantial
44. Policeman, sometimes
47. Hypnosis ender
48. ½ fl. oz.
49. Scoot
50. Party giver
51. Doomed, slangily

DOWN

1. What Benjamin was accused of stealing (Genesis 44:1–2)
2. Hoopla
3. Pained cry
4. "_____ the idea"
5. Abound
6. "That's _____ need"
7. People that Joseph's brothers sold him to (Genesis 37:27)
8. St. closest to Cuba
9. Applied for candidacy
10. Clothing rack letters
13. High-fat fruit
16. Pharaoh put 30-year-old Joseph in charge of the _____ (Genesis 41:45–48)
19. Avoid on purpose
21. Sound from a merino
22. Former U.N. chief

24. From Dublin
25. "Pharaoh said unto Joseph, I have dreamed a dream, and there is none that can _____ it" (Genesis 41:15)
28. Go-_____
30. Fashion magazine
32. _____-mo

36. Kind of acid in protein
39. Cole and Turner
40. Tree ornament shapes
41. Labor Day mo.
42. Volcanic fallout
43. Dorm VIPs
45. Rap music article
46. Autobahn hazard

Answers on page 185.

Parable Anagrams

ACROSS

1. Litigators org.
4. Comic-book curse
8. Long sighs
12. Parable about a plant that was fruitless three years straight (anagram of ART BEING FREER)
13. Compass dir.
14. Beach bucket
15. Cheeky tykes
16. Ocean eagles
18. Verso's mate
20. Actress Wood
23. Geologist's suffix
25. Grant-providing org.
26. Old Testament mount
28. Parable about making excuses (anagram of GUEST RAPPER)
30. Be ravenous
31. Dorm figs.
33. Glutton
34. Parable about handling the entrusted funds (anagram of NET SALT)
37. Bizarre, slangily
40. Spreads, as seeds
41. Squeezed (out)
43. Body sci.
46. Suit go-with
47. Parable about an inappropriately dressed man at the banquet (anagram of EDGED SNUG WITS)
48. Calendar squares
49. Spanish direction
50. CIA, once

DOWN

1. Missing from school
2. City Arabs rebuilt
3. Don't exist
4. Airline abbr.
5. Biochem. messenger
6. Excited
7. Mah-jongg piece
8. Working or fighting
9. Suit holder
10. Cool, formerly
11. Part of some sonnets

17. Better balanced
19. Wrist-related
21. Parable about a substance that a woman took and hid in three measures of meal (anagram of EEL VAN)
22. Straying dev's companion?
24. Ancient mariner
26. Personal vibe
27. Certain recesses
28. Early Pontiac muscle car
29. Unkempt

30. Like good servants in the Bible
32. Look at critically
34. Salad servers
35. Inaccurate
36. Dunderheads
38. Bookies know them
39. Retired bodybuilder Frank
42. Mauna _____, Hawaii
44. Insurance co. employee
45. Calendar abbr.

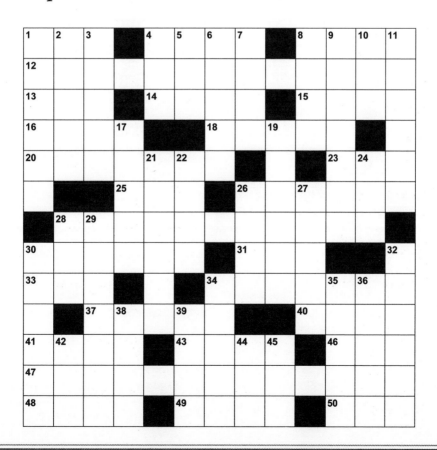

Answers on page 186.

Noah's Ark

ACROSS

1. Concealed from view
4. Interim measure
10. Certain to get
12. Billing unit, often
13. Spicy sandwich filler
14. Romantic gift
15. What the returning 40-Down had in its beak (Genesis 8:10–11)
18. Like mutton
19. Lots of ozs.
20. Fry corrugation
22. Impolite expression
25. Verb ender?
26. Deluge refuge
28. Mineral dug from a mine
29. Twining plant
32. Ornate tea vessel
35. Rabbit action
37. The 46th president
38. Noah became a father at this age (Genesis 5:32)
41. A lot
43. Slammers
44. Mission-scrapping words
45. Does laps in a pool
46. Small strong canvas used in stormy weather
47. Heat source

DOWN

1. American wildcat
2. Join a teleconference
3. Remove a connection
4. Any number of
5. Warbling sound
6. Short pithy expression
7. Blockhead
8. Neighbor of Switz.
9. Noah was called "a _____ of righteousness" (2 Peter 2:5)
11. Brazilian slum
13. The former _____ Union
16. Early Scandinavian
17. Outward movement
20. God established it with Noah (Genesis 9:8–12)
21. Triage locales, briefly
23. Valentine senders

24. Large hoist

27. Traditional Japanese drama

30. Some casual wear

31. Carpooling car, for short

33. Half notes

34. Bizarre in the extreme

36. Coke rival

38. Stodgy old-timer

39. Roaring wind sound

40. One of the two animals sent out in search of a dry land (Genesis 8:6–10)

42. Bare crag

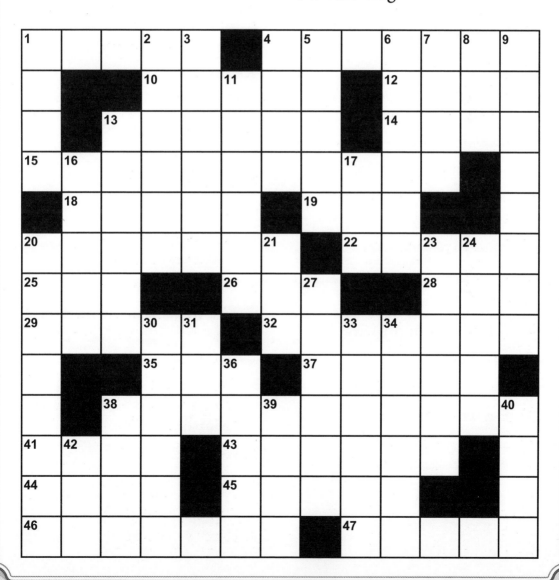

Answers on page 186.

Workers in the Vineyard

ACROSS

1. "So the last _____, and the first last" (Matthew 20:16)
10. Appear to observe many
11. Part of a geom. line
12. Continental abbr.
13. Hoist
15. Plain _____
16. Liveliness of mind
17. Mascara mishap
19. Knock unconscious
20. Like some high hairdos
24. Manually shred
28. Chem-lab procedure
29. Deer kin
30. Jungle climbing plant
31. Like commuter towns
32. Tijuana trio
34. State of western U.S.
37. English regatta town
41. Deeply sarcastic
42. Old car, maybe
44. Sopranos' group?
45. Curve of a sort
46. Deal starter
47. The time the last were hired (Matthew 20:6)

DOWN

1. Has an appointment with
2. Relief
3. United States: abbr.
4. Law sch. exam
5. Casino act
6. Cast out from the body
7. Peruse prose
8. Made vocal music
9. Part of a grove
14. Laborers' workplace (Matthew 20:2)
15. Lesser partner
16. The householder made the payout _____ for everyone (Matthew 20:12)
18. The workers "_____ against the goodman of the house" (Matthew 20:11)
19. Hog enclosures
21. Air-in-tire letters
22. New Deal org.
23. Hirer's posting

25. Postal acronym
26. Neighbor of Can.
27. The amount of money every worker received (Matthew 20:1–13)
33. All gone, dinnerwise
34. Family crest inscription
35. Env. science
36. Intuitive feeling
37. _____ browns
38. Title fish in a 2003 movie
39. Place, in legalese
40. MIT grad.
43. Post-Q run

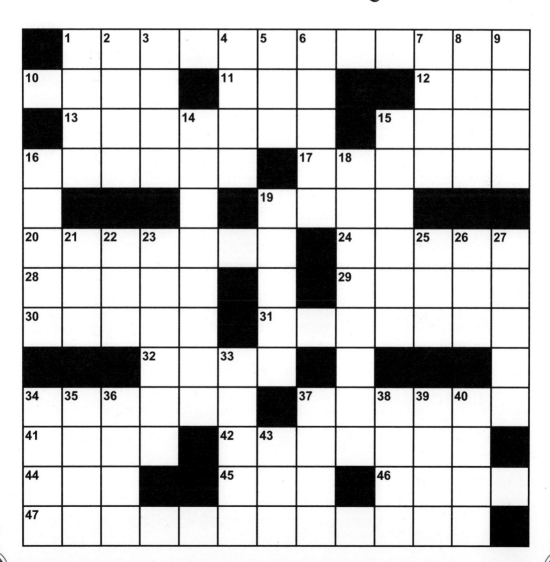

Answers on page 186.

Esther

ACROSS

1. Esther's original name, meaning "the myrtle" (Esther 2:7)
8. Reward, as a dog
11. Become slick, in a way
12. Metallic element
15. As given above
16. Verbalizer
17. Hang downward
19. Behaving properly
20. _____ rule (ordinarily)
21. Ship's debris
23. Inspected
25. Memo-heading abbr.
26. Arrow shooter
28. "_____ man of my word"
30. Large ratites
32. Humiliating person
35. Academic aides, briefly
37. Had coming
39. Early Mongolian
41. Banes
43. Gorges
45. Not taken in by consumers
46. Heroic works
47. Narrow sailing rte.
48. He told 1-Across about the plot to assassinate 20-Down (Esther 2:21–23)

DOWN

1. Stashed in a safe place
2. Amino _____
3. Derogate
4. Garage dweller
5. Makes fun of
6. Kleptomaniac film monkey
7. Bandleader's cry
8. Holiday which commemorates the saving of the Jewish people from Haman (Esther 9:24–27)
9. "Got two fives for _____?"
10. 1-Across asked everyone to fast for _____ (Esther 4:16)
13. Train sched. list
14. First lady before Jill
18. Common person
20. The king whose order Vashti the queen disobeyed (Esther 1:9–19)

22. Olfactory perceptions

24. Aerial

27. Make an edge sharper

29. Audio product manufacturer

31. Rubbed off the page

32. Less damp

33. Plant grown for sugar

34. Pertinent, in Latin

36. Betel nut tree

38. Certain wedding guest

40. Adhesive strip

42. Cone head?

44. Fed. support program

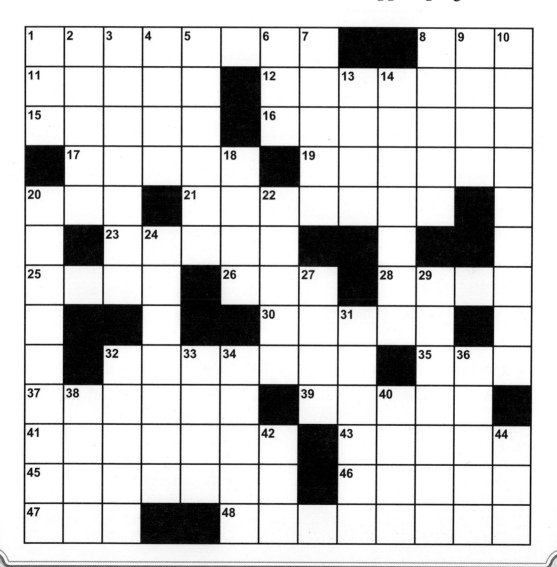

Answers on page 186.

David's Prayers

ACROSS

1. Word found in every one of Psalm 72's first three verses
11. Blessing-curse link
12. TV channel
13. Terminer's partner
14. Bellyache
17. Addition column
18. Prepare to pray
19. Atoll, essentially
21. What the Lord sent unto his people (Psalm 111:9)
24. Ceremonial display
27. Fine, in France
28. Ant-thy joiner
29. Hails
31. Winter autobahn hazard
32. Anklebone-related
34. Pitcher Saberhagen
35. Counsellor and conspirator against whom David prays (2 Samuel 15:31)
38. Greek holiday island
39. Equivalent
43. Bulldoze
45. Windpipes (Lat.)
47. Promote vigorously
48. Macbeth preposition
49. Natl. park campers
50. David pleaded with God to be kept from them (Psalm 17:9)

DOWN

1. Terrain formation higher than him that he wanted to be lead to (Psalm 61:2)
2. Anemia treatment
3. Ready
4. Silk netting
5. Smog watchdog gp.
6. Chilling, say
7. Comment
8. Glittery cosmetic
9. Capitol VIP
10. Alums-to-be, briefly
15. Busted party
16. Roaming type
20. Tachometer nos.
22. Garfield's pal
23. Crane construction

24. Falafel holder
25. Aquarium fish
26. Populous Arizona county
29. Cowardly Lion portrayer
30. Floating up above
33. Put in a footlocker
34. Not so great
36. Blender speed
37. Show host

40. Polo of "Meet the Parents"
41. Hiding place where David was praying to be delivered from his persecutors (Psalm 142:1)
42. Big name in oil
43. Dissertation finisher
44. Caustic chemical
46. Prince Valiant's firstborn

Answers on page 187.

Mary & Martha

ACROSS

1. One of the sisters "sat at Jesus' feet, and _____" (Luke 10:39)
11. Type of opera
12. Latest fad
13. Ball raiser
14. Lhasa _____ (dog breed)
15. Horrific smell
16. Potent finish?
17. Neckwear fixer
19. String-quartet member
21. Lightens
23. Ointment
27. They might be nervous
30. The sisters who offered hospitality to Jesus (Luke 10:38–42)
33. Words on a sale tag
34. Sent along
35. Art-studio solvent
37. Teeny-_____
39. Oxygen-loving organism
43. Swiss stream
44. Apple variety?
47. Is in debt to
48. _____-fi
49. Evening, informally
50. Red planet
51. Jesus said Mary had chosen "_____" (Luke 10:42)

DOWN

1. Northern Arizona native
2. Hassle-free state
3. Per unit, informally
4. Lecture badly
5. Was stricken with
6. "Can _____ now?"
7. "Lord, dost thou not care that my sister hath left me to _____ alone?" (Luke 10:40)
8. Sloth
9. Genuine
10. Creme-creme center
11. Orange type
18. Pelvis bones
20. IV part?
22. Tennis legend Agassi
24. Bana follower

25. Reference points
26. Boxer Mike
28. Writer Gossett
29. Remorseful feeling
31. Hung over
32. On the quieter side
36. Resting
37. Were, biblically

38. Every one of a number
40. Capital city of Italia
41. Man _____ (all-time great racehorse)
42. Unibrowed Muppet
45. Part of a famous Neapolitan song title
46. From _____ Z

Answers on page 187.

Verses About Prayer

ACROSS

1. "Continue in prayer, and watch in the same with _____" (Colossians 4:2)
11. Kett of comics
12. Beatty of "Deliverance"
13. Sorrowful sort
14. Processing time meas.
15. Artist Watteau
17. Show a response
19. Complete
23. Japanese hostess
26. Self-reflective question
27. Repugnant shout
29. Famed furrier
30. Casual shirt, casually
31. Cosmologist Hubble
33. Putrefy
34. Noted chipmaker
36. Ristorante ending
37. Blissful sigh
38. Kansas natives
40. Big Board competitor
42. Freshwater diving bird
44. Less serene
46. "Girls" creator Dunham
49. Die down
50. Marine abbr.
51. "_____ the Lord and his strength, _____ his face continually" (1 Chronicles 16:11)
52. "... and watching thereunto with all _____ and supplication for all saints" (Ephesians 6:18)

DOWN

1. "Watch and pray, that ye enter not into _____: the spirit indeed is willing, but the flesh is weak" (Matthew 26:41)
2. Elevations, for short
3. Had food
4. Cheesy snack
5. Wolfed (down)
6. _____ pool
7. Luggage attachment
8. Eye inflammation
9. Convent occupant
10. Grand, moneywise

16. South Pacific region
18. "And suddenly there was a great _____, so that the foundations of the prison were shaken" (Acts 16:26–33)
20. Chilling signs
21. Michelangelo marble
22. Opinion checks
24. Classic violin, briefly
25. Disturbance

28. Armistice Day confl.
32. Stimulate
35. More yolkish
39. Water near Notre Dame
41. Cantina condiment
43. A Cleaver, familiarly
44. Afternoon indulgence
45. Celebratory piece
47. Poetic dusk
48. Tokyo-based tech giant

Answers on page 187.

The Resurrection

ACROSS

1. Letters of uncertainty
3. DC donor
6. Furtive glance
10. "And ____ he shall [21-Down]" (Matthew 20:19)
12. Toronto's province
13. Protective shield (var.)
14. Corleone family head
15. Furry adoptees
16. Like a facial cavity
19. Horror movie character
22. Pass the bouncer
23. Unwelcome eyeful
24. The Sun City
26. Anxious feeling
30. Blind as ____
32. Tanned skin
33. Maker of riding gear
37. Chocolate ingredient
38. Croft of the catacombs
39. Lake formed by glaciation
41. Straitlaced
42. Summertime beverage
44. "Jesus was risen early ____ of the week" (Mark 16:9)
45. Martial follower
46. General name in takeout?
47. Was the boss of

DOWN

1. Mary Magdalene saw them next to the body of Jesus (John 20:11–13)
2. Bar assoc. member
3. Dire straits
4. Back ____ again
5. Pick
6. Get ready
7. Lawn-trimming targets
8. Piaf of song
9. Quaint
11. Capital of Cuba
17. Onetime buyer of "Time"
18. Slowly enjoy a coffee
20. 40-day long time of repentance
21. "For as yet they knew not the scripture, that he must ____ from the dead" (John 20:9)

23. Rounded ear projection

25. Greek island sausages

27. Fleming of "Spellbound"

28. Singer Damone

29. Pre-1868 Tokyo

31. Visual creator

34. Dominant, among animals

35. Challenging one?

36. Float aimlessly

37. Confession of faith

40. The only King James Bible book where the word "Easter" is used

43. Norse equivalent of Mars

Answers on page 187.

The Good Samaritan

ACROSS

1. Condition that 24-Down left the man in after inflicting 35-Down on him (Luke 10:30)
8. Newborn child
11. Acting Stephen
12. Some kinfolk
13. Derisive shout
14. Anticavity org.
15. Dry biscuit
17. Elephant flappers
18. What the traveling Samaritan showed (Luke 10:37)
20. "Believe _____ not!"
22. Apportion
25. Potent ending?
28. Illegal firing
29. Fireworks reaction
30. Go on all fours
31. Dinar spender
32. Stomach acid, chemically
33. Generally recognized
36. "Science Guy" Bill
37. Busy airport
39. Christmas rendition
41. Fancy farewell
43. Serving Nastase
46. Person in the inn who was given two pence to take care of the unfortunate one (Luke 10:35)
48. Act immorally
49. Rough waters
50. Verbal noun
51. Prison break, e.g.
52. Emeritus, briefly
53. What both the priest and the Levite did instead of helping (Luke 10:31–32)

DOWN

2. Atlas datum
3. Creepy gaze
4. Persian tongue
5. Make beloved
6. Parable's main character and the 46-Across
7. Adored
8. Green gemstone
9. Tempe sch.

10. Domesticated ox
13. City where the one who fell among 24-Down was headed (Luke 10:30)
16. Foolish
19. Dog-like
21. Conversed
23. Museum deal
24. Ones who stripped the raiment and physically hurt their victim (Luke 10:30)
26. Primitive (prefix)
27. In _____-land
34. Million preceder
35. Injuries caused by the robbers (Luke 10:30)
38. Designated
40. Glove fabric
42. Has run out
44. Desired role
45. Poetic unit
46. Biblical mount
47. NYPD figure

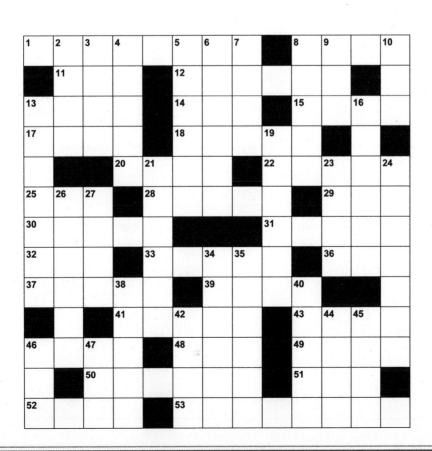

Answers on page 188.

"J" Names in the Bible

ACROSS

1. Chinese perfume stick
5. Foster son of the comics
8. Fiction's opposite
12. Art Deco legend
13. Classic 8-bit console: abbr.
14. Unknown source, for short
15. Peace disturbance
16. Surname of Judas, "the son of Simon" (John 6:71)
18. Marry
19. Singer LeAnn
20. Earth's natural orbiter
21. German opera composer
23. GIs on foot
24. The successor of Moses (Deuteronomy 31:23)
27. Forest flautist
29. Bigger butte
31. Pauses in hostilities
33. Anatomical pouch
35. Like Copernicus
37. "Little Women" sister
38. Ram of the firmament
39. Coop flier

41. Friend of David (1 Samuel 18:1–4)
43. Pierce with a blade
44. Seeks, as permission
45. CNBC news item
46. Irked reaction
47. Iconic 1990s computer game
48. Satan put his faith to a great test
49. Served a winner, in tennis

DOWN

1. One of the Major Prophets of the Old Testament
2. Prayer (archaic)
3. Visit briefly
4. Serious about
5. Tropical American cuckoos
6. Fixes, as a seam
7. Situation Room gp.
8. Vegetable meals
9. Big-eyed Asian cartoons
10. Dove imitator
11. They cause blowups: abbr.
17. Has words (with)

22. Wistful phrase
24. Legal scholar
25. Weighty obligation
26. Mother of Miriam, Aaron and Moses (Numbers 26:59)
28. Minimally
30. Sanitized

32. Inexpensive, slangily
34. Laid back
35. Written unimaginatively
36. Piggy noises
37. Seaport of Iraq
38. Caught in _____
40. Condescending sort
42. Pre-K letters

1	2	3	4		5	6	7		8	9	10	11
12					13				14			
15					16		17					
18								19				
20						21	22					
23				24	25							26
		27	28				29			30		
			31			32				33	34	
	35	36							37			
38					39	40						
41				42				43				
44				45				46				
47				48				49				

Answers on page 188.

Elijah & Elisha

ACROSS

1. He brought the rain after lengthy drought (1 Kings 18:41–45)
6. "Ironic" singer Morissette
11. Actor Aykroyd
12. Hollywood force, in brief
14. Eat main meal
15. Spill out
17. Inst. of learning
18. Symbolizes the passing of prophetic authority (2 Kings 2:11–14)
20. Constrictor reptiles
21. Beat in a race
22. Attain
23. Low dam
25. Food that the ravens brought 1-Across (1 Kings 17:6)
30. Bacon go-with
31. Golden Triangle land
32. Use a recorder
35. Senior lobby org.
36. 1-Across "went up by a _____ into heaven" (2 Kings 2:11)
40. Bedrock barker
42. Urban renewal targets
44. At a tie score
45. Bit of angling gear
46. Thurman of "Pulp Fiction"
47. Marsh growths
48. Proof of consent

DOWN

1. A small whirl of water
2. "Love Story" composer
3. Imminent
4. Skin-soothing ingredients
5. Have an adverse effect on
6. Lymphoid throat masses
7. Full price payer, usually
8. Bay Area NFLer
9. Noodle suffix
10. Some fractions
13. Tour operator
16. Country in West Africa
19. Stomping ground
20. Raise the _____
22. Receding seas
23. Gamblers

24. Grade sch. class
26. Cheese counter
27. Southwestern grassy plain
28. Aural membrane
29. Pacifying gesture
33. Had a title
34. Beach sandal

35. Walk down the _____
37. Caustic agent
38. Opposite of rejoice
39. "The wolf _____ the door"
41. Product add-on?
43. Sony Music competitor

Answers on page 188.

A Prayer of Repentance

ACROSS

1. David prayed to have them blot out (Psalm 51:9)
9. One of the kings of Judah
10. Barracks boss, for short
11. Bleak genre
14. Machine parts
15. Movie set VIP
16. Jai _____ (indoor sport)
17. Much more complicated
19. DC group
20. Brewing rebellion
22. Gas pump stat
26. Ruined, to a Brit
29. Tourist's query
30. Ornate tapestry
31. Acidity indicator
33. Plant David wanted to be purged with (Psalm 51:7)
34. Impenetrable to light
36. Bucks, perhaps
39. Someone who intentionally sends a weakened soldier to the forefront of the hottest battle (2 Samuel 11:13–17)
43. Pop singer Halliwell
44. Above (poetic)
45. Actress Petty
46. Tony winner Kazan
47. Great expanse
48. Ultimate
49. David asked God to create it in him (Psalm 51:10)

DOWN

1. Cue-following comment
2. Canceled, to NASA
3. Part of MIT
4. Soulless water nymph
5. Comparatively chilly
6. Spanish soccer legend Fernando
7. Successful lawmakers
8. Alone
9. "For I _____ my transgressions: and my sin is ever before me" (Psalm 51:3)
12. Actor McShane
13. David pleaded to the Lord to renew it within him (Psalm 51:10)

18. Auto garage job
21. Fixed, in a way
23. Greek X
24. Holiday in Asia
25. Heraldry-related
27. 1040 reviewer: abbr.
28. Northeast Thai tongue
32. Triangular fried pastry

33. Holler of triumph
35. Esther or Jezebel's title
37. Elongated fish
38. Bana of movies
40. Scat master Fitzgerald
41. Copy a lion
42. While lead-in

Answers on page 188.

Biblical Mountains

ACROSS

1. Applications to sprains
7. Mount from which Moses saw the Promised Land (Deuteronomy 34:1)
9. Bonn article
10. Thread-spinning Fate
12. Clean-air agcy.
13. User-friendly
14. Certain tourney overseer
16. Where Abraham was to sacrifice Isaac (Genesis 22:2)
19. Ida. neighbor
20. Germany's Merkel
22. Alloys resembling gold
26. _____ flask
27. Drone regulator, in brief
28. Matter in law
30. Depot datum
31. Suitable for the chorus
34. Nightclub show
37. Remain in hiding
39. City, informally
40. Where Elijah challenged the prophets of Baal (1 Kings 18:1–46)
45. Prez's backup
46. Country singer Chelsea
47. Perfume label word
48. Sidestepped
49. Fed. stipend
50. The peak originally inhabited by Horites (Genesis 14:6)
51. Creative types

DOWN

1. Same as mentioned
2. Crime bigwig
3. Jacob's twin
4. Like a vinegar radical
5. Beauty
6. Not bad, not good
7. Legal infancy
8. The mountains _____ upon which the Ark rested (Genesis 8:4)
11. Banks of fashion fame
15. Masticator

17. Certain global political concept: abbr.
18. Political poll abbr.
21. Flight-board posting
22. "Jesus went unto the mount ____" (John 8:1)
23. Indian dignitary
24. Words of defiance
25. Brief time period
29. Specialty chef
32. Amorous runaway
33. Pointer's pronoun
35. Nobel-winning chancellor
36. Like a pocket dict.
38. Seattle Storms org.
41. Mock fanfare word
42. Disorderly accumulation
43. Toward the sunrise
44. San ____, Argentina

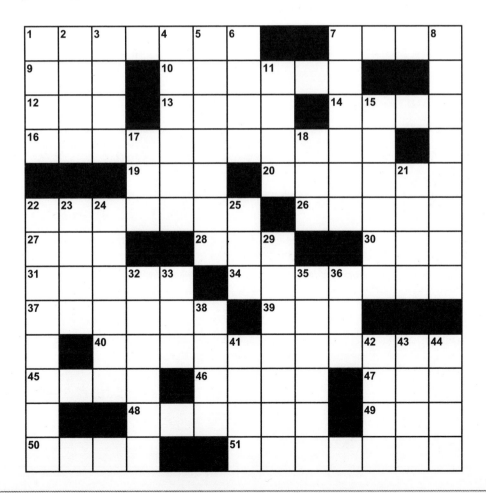

Answers on page 189.

Isaiah

ACROSS

1. Common paella ingredients
6. Raisin cakes
11. Datebook abbr.
12. Ideal
13. More solemn
16. Support person
17. "In quietness and in _____ shall be your [10-Down]" (Isaiah 30:15)
18. Ticket word
19. Pixielike
22. Shout upon an arrival
25. Calculating the sum of
26. _____ culpa
27. Bill for merchandise: abbr.
28. RR crossing
29. Weasel's relative
32. Prophetic Old Testament book
35. Perfume from rose petals
36. Mane
37. "The _____ shall be upon his shoulder" (Isaiah 9:6)
41. Starving
44. Mate's replies
45. Deeply sincere
46. Full of meaning
47. Clues, to detectives
48. Dangers

DOWN

1. Gender abbr.
2. Involved with
3. Stretch over
4. Suppress
5. Binge in a mall
6. Fixed firmly
7. Off the beaten track
8. Breakfast companion?
9. Winning serve
10. "But they that wait upon the Lord shall renew their _____" (Isaiah 40:31)
14. Schiaparelli competitor
15. Enter furtively
20. Pacific vacation island
21. Highlander of old

22. "A virgin shall conceive, and bear a son, and shall call his name _____" (Isaiah 7:14)

23. Essential part

24. "Shall the lame man leap as an _____, and the tongue of the dumb sing" (Isaiah 35:6)

25. Source of some tweets

30. Random scrap

31. Washes away at

33. Calculator function

34. Historic Spanish fleet

36. Toffee bar choice

38. One who observes

39. Desire

40. Vanilla extract amts.

42. No, to a kilt wearer

43. Bro. in a monastery

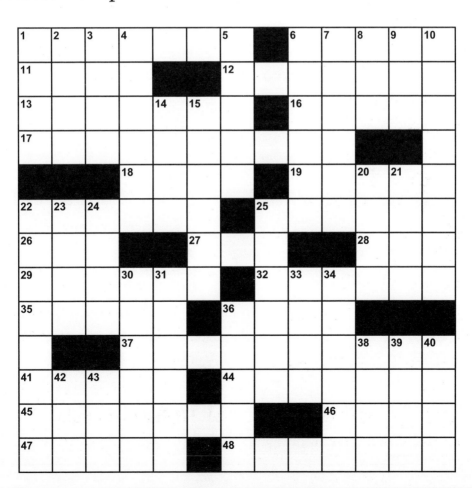

Answers on page 189.

Bible Animals

ACROSS

1. Jonah spent three days and nights in the belly of _____ (Jonah 1:17)
10. More than hesitant
11. Island in Ionian Sea
14. Soft palate neighbor
15. Rock from space
16. Land document
17. Complete a deal
19. Coastal county of England
21. It comes before quattro
22. Bachelorette
23. Venomous creature that "came out of the heat" and bit Apostle Paul (Acts 28:3)
25. Bedtime story
26. Soybean in soup
27. Anthony Hopkins's role in "Thor"
29. Passageway for Santa
31. Galley toiler
33. Starter for many Spanish city names
34. Plum's center
35. Cable service
38. Had a tendency
41. Something extra
42. Staring lecherously
43. Deschanel of "Bones"
45. "This I Promise You" band
46. Oak containers
47. "The east wind brought _____", the eighth plague of Egypt (Exodus 10:13)

DOWN

2. Affixes, in a way
3. Traverses
4. French for "water of life"
5. Icel. surrounder
6. Pointer's word
7. Emotional public display
8. Chili peppers, informally
9. Bird used as an offering (Luke 2:23–24)
12. Actor elected president
13. Pivotal
15. Spinal cord substance

16. King Darius condemned Daniel to death by throwing him into the _____ (Daniel 6:9–16)
18. AAA option
20. Greek characters
24. Examining, with over
25. Custardy dessert
26. Strong
28. Bank trans.
30. Suit sizes
32. Coy conclusion?
34. Smidgen
36. Most nutrient-dense egg parts
37. Hush-hush hookup
39. Navel discovery
40. Twenties art form
44. Jobs and Wozniak creation, briefly

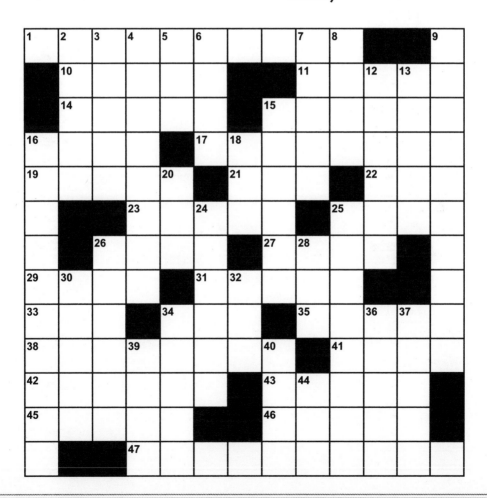

Answers on page 189.

The Unforgiving Servant

ACROSS

1. The lord loosed the servant and "____" the 24-Down (Matthew 18:27)
10. Place for a belt
11. Large guest room in an Albanian traditional house
12. ____ Gay (WWII bomber)
13. With no fixed pitch
15. Opposite direction of 27-Across
16. Crane construction
17. Sierra ____
19. Mordant
21. Freebie
24. FedEx competitor
25. Mid-size Kia
27. Chem. suffix
29. Be in accord
31. GPS determination
32. Fillet, say
34. Settle the bill
36. Last stroke, usually
37. Dying fire feature
40. Detroit dud
42. Mate's address
45. Famous Frazier foe
46. Vernacular
48. Broadband choice
49. Eastern Med. land
50. Great sorrow
51. "The lord of that servant was moved with ____" (Matthew 18:27)

DOWN

1. Law-breaking cost
2. Makes a pick
3. Geometric suffix
4. One-named British singer
5. Dark side Darth
6. Previously cut, as timber
7. Six-legged crawler
8. Cut some blades
9. A servant said: "Lord, ____ with me, and I will pay thee all" (Matthew 18:26)
10. The amount to be repaid (Matthew 18:28)

14. Jazz setting?
18. Tubular instrument
20. Scottish kinsmen
22. Smoothly ingratiating
23. UFC sport
24. Money owed
26. _____ Le Pew of cartoons
28. Modern, in Germany
30. Thousands of slang

33. Title role for a tenor
35. Former BP gas brand
38. Press
39. Praise or glorify
41. Carpe _____
43. "It's _____ party system"
44. Quantum particle
45. Easy as _____
47. Robinson of song

Answers on page 189.

Walking on Water

ACROSS

1. Chicago L, for one
6. Periodicals, briefly
10. Jesus comforted his people: "Be of good cheer: it is I; _____" (Mark 6:50)
12. Make even shorter
13. Bit of truth
14. Modify
16. Capital of Azerbaijan
18. Brand of pads
20. Campbell of fashion
22. Amazon's virtual assistant
24. Inert medication
27. _____-à-_____
28. Many city layouts
30. Oxford instructor
31. Start, as an adventure
33. Got down on one knee
34. Boors
36. Japanese drama form
37. "Oh, my"
40. Overtake
43. _____-null (math figure)
45. Restores a house
46. The disciples "were troubled, saying, _____; and they cried out for fear" (Matthew 14:26)
47. Grabs a snack
48. Oregon Trail city

DOWN

1. Shout made by Peter when he started drowning (Matthew 14:29–31)
2. Least intelligent
3. Offender, to a cop
4. Author Blyton
5. Any of the Caesars
6. Maker: abbr.
7. Like some numerals
8. Greek earth goddess
9. Go under (like a 42-Down)
11. Hallowed by antiquity
15. Use as a resource
17. Jesus "cometh unto them, walking _____" (Mark 6:48)
19. Actress Lena of "Alias"
21. Ski _____

23. Farm-related prefix

25. Lacking teeth

26. Cord worn as a necktie

29. Golf course areas

32. First in order of birth

35. Diagonal sail support

38. Castle entrance

39. Inter follower

41. Dynamic introduction?

42. "Jesus constrained his disciples to get into a _____" (Matthew 14:22)

44. Faux _____

Answers on page 190.

Paul the Apostle

ACROSS

1. Half prefix
5. Paul's contributions to the New Testament
11. Utterly absurd
12. Faith, _____, and 8-Down
13. Digital vid. format
14. "Nightmare" street
16. Big beauty brand
17. A few feet from
19. Cardinal point
20. "Paul, a servant of Jesus Christ, called to be an _____" (Romans 1:1)
22. Grotto isle of Italy
25. Liturgical hymn of praise to God
29. Abbr. on an old TV
30. Explorer of Canada's coast
32. Center opening?
33. Indian chief
35. Village cousins
37. One seizing power
40. Embassy waver
43. Building for public worship
45. _____ Island
46. Divided country: abbr.
47. Angelic symbol
49. Blemish
50. Inhabitant
51. Paul was one before conversion
52. Turns blue, in a way

DOWN

1. Paul was blinded by Jesus on the road to _____ (Acts 9:1–9)
2. Claimed psychic skill
3. Demeanor
4. Ready to drive
5. First month, in Madrid
6. Mammal coats
7. Became more genial
8. Feeling elaborately described by Paul
9. Collection of verse
10. En route
15. Words often framed
18. Zeniths

21. Another name for each of the 5-Across
23. Word of understanding
24. Enlisted mil. rank
26. "Yuck!"
27. Bygone TV channel
28. Special assignments, biblically
31. Without self-control
34. Affectionate sort
36. Glamorous tropical flower
38. Half of a state name
39. Make into baby food
40. Wing motion
41. Scottish aquatic locale
42. Dancer Pavlova
44. Fuzzy
48. Bruce with the kicks

Answers on page 190.

Bible Prophecies

ACROSS

1. Rising of Christ from the dead as prophesied by Hosea
10. Actress Thurman
11. Love, Latin-style
12. Biathlon gliders
14. Scoreless
15. Bell-ringing company
16. Biblical travelers to Bethlehem
17. Broadway legend Stritch
19. Mark or John, say
21. "Behold, a virgin shall conceive, and bear a son, and shall call his name _____" (Isaiah 7:14)
23. Project closing?
24. Skype technology, briefly
25. Scrooge's look
27. Declares, in comics
29. Contract
31. Preceded, with "to"
34. Editorial command, briefly
36. Approx. repair cost
39. Judas's disgraceful act predicted in Psalm 41

41. Make preparations
43. Arctic topper
45. Racing champ Luyendyk
46. Woodwind instrument
48. Aesopian insect
49. Latvian city
50. Orchestra sect.
51. Campground letters
52. Every person testifying untruths against Jesus (Psalm 35:11)

DOWN

1. Germanic mark
2. Actor Estevez
3. Deli display
4. Baltimore footballers
5. Alt-rock subgenre
6. Savory rice porridge
7. Slangy doctrines
8. Striped rainforest critter
9. Brexit politician Farage
13. After opening the seventh seal this is going to last half an hour (Revelation 8:1)
15. Comp. of stories

18. Coerce

20. Couturier Cassini

22. Not censored

24. "They gave me also gall for my meat; and in my thirst they gave me _____ to drink" (Psalm 69:21)

26. Tint again

28. Asian ox

30. Cookie

32. Overthrow

33. A _____ (deductive)

35. Peruvian plains

37. Finishing stroke

38. Subarctic forest

40. Certain pilot

42. Type of number

44. Sch. auxiliaries

47. Incidentally, in texts

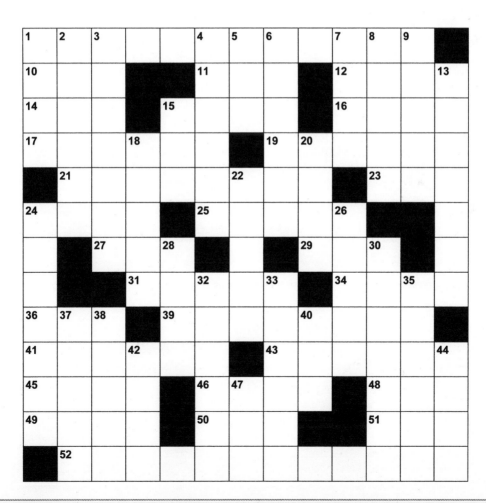

Answers on page 190.

Jesus Heals a Blind Beggar

ACROSS

1. 37-Across was one
6. Indian spice mix
11. "About _____" (2002 movie)
12. Ocean State sch.
14. _____-deucey (game)
15. Radio-active one?
16. Halfway prefix
17. Suburban pride
18. "Jesus Christ, the _____, the son of Abraham" (Matthew 1:1)
20. Hershiser of the diamond
21. Pirate booty holder
25. Grayheads
30. "And he cried, saying, Jesus, thou [18-Across], _____" (Luke 18:38)
32. Soccer team count
33. A symbol of Christianity
34. Guarded
37. The blind son of Timaeus (Mark 10:46)
41. Brazilian sports legend
42. Hawaiian necklace
43. El _____ (Pacific current)
45. "_____ the sick, cleanse the lepers" (Matthew 10:8)
46. Tolkien tree being
47. Lay _____ the line
48. Conformed
49. Those who abhor

DOWN

1. Spinal pain
2. Fall back, water-wise
3. Makes a move
4. Sandwich with tzatziki
5. Hearsay
6. Piano student's key note
7. Surrealist Dalí
8. Berry in many smoothies
9. Licentious
10. Objectivist writer Rand
13. Abundant
19. Someone else did it
22. Evil computer of moviedom
23. Abel's mother
24. In a harsh way
26. French high school

27. Ambient music giant Brian
28. Apt. ad stat
29. Therapy appointments
31. Stored, as grain
35. Prayer conclusion
36. "Receive thy sight: thy _____ hath saved thee" (Luke 18:42)

37. British network, informally, with "the"
38. Wings, in Latin
39. Type of pricing
40. Safari destination
41. Hanoi bowlful
44. Likewise not

1	2	3	4		5		6		7	8	9	10
11					12	13			14			
15					16				17			
		18		19								
			20									
21	22	23	24				25	26		27	28	29
30					31							
32							33					
					34	35	36					
	37	38							39	40		
41				42				43		44	
45				46				47			
48					49						

Answers on page 190.

More Psalms

ACROSS

1. "_____, all ye people; shout unto God with the voice of triumph" (Psalm 47:1)
9. Expert's antithesis
10. Hi-tech scanner: abbr.
11. Formal-affair wear
14. Disorganized mound
17. Ballet classroom fixture
18. Around a line of symmetry
20. David asked God to forgive him _____ (Psalm 25:18)
22. Pop diva Celine
25. State games
26. Big Ten inits.
27. Metal plate
29. Memorable span
30. Wood-shaping tools
32. Political doctrines
33. "I will say of the Lord, He is my refuge and _____" (Psalm 91:2)
36. Acclimate
37. Tenth
41. Forget-me-_____
43. Property receivers, at law
45. Place for travelers
46. Famed Dadaist
47. "The Lord knoweth the _____, that they are vanity" (Psalm 94:11)

DOWN

1. Salad inventor Bob
2. "_____ Land" (2016 musical)
3. Distant
4. Cosmopolitan's opposite
5. Big mo. for costume sales
6. Biblical name
7. Dumbstruck
8. Crime scene matter
12. Juice name prefix
13. Expel from country
15. Upper-crust types
16. Successfully imitate
19. Currently airs
21. Expected behavior
22. Turkish long robe with sleeves
23. British sentence starter

24. Set of matching clothes
27. Center of the Incan empire
28. Stars in Kansas's motto
31. Main island of Japan
32. "Beauty _____ the eye of the beholder"
34. Ignited anew

35. Writer of short letters
38. Group playing a game
39. Jealous wife of Zeus
40. Sports cable chan.
42. "Now I understand!"
44. Weigh-_____ (bout rituals)

Answers on page 191.

Ten Talents

ACROSS

1. Andean camelids
7. Farmers, at times
12. Big occasion
13. Demonic
14. What the most successful servant did, talent-wise (Matthew 25:20)
16. "There's _____ in team"
17. Mrs. Victor Laszlo
18. Fish trouble
20. Trade goods for cash
21. Courtroom pledge
22. Very slick
25. Tupperware cover
27. What the indolent laborer did that angered his master when he returned (Matthew 25:25)
31. Certain numero
32. Society peon
33. Cooking aids
35. Furrowed fruit
38. Compass letters
39. Pass the threshold
40. Up to the time of
42. His superior expected the wicked servant to put his funds to them (Matthew 25:27)
46. Transaction, contract or bargain that brings profits
47. Canadian movie award
48. Leave unaffected
49. Stable guy?

DOWN

2. Building block
3. Benefited
4. Puzzle-ster link
5. Alabama city founded as a private village
6. Ancient burial stone
7. Happens to, old-style
8. Bird prefix
9. Tyler of "The Leftovers"
10. Hollywood's Verdugo
11. Quality of the worker who was given one coin (Matthew 25:26)
15. Hi-speed connection

16. Biblical ark builder

19. Singer Waters

21. Dump feature

23. Emulate the one of the three who didn't earn anything

24. An added quantity, as per investment

26. Encroaches

28. More or less

29. Breathing channel

30. Scream

33. Above the rest

34. Major town in northern England

36. Indian tourist spot

37. Slang

41. Comment with a nod

43. Ballot marks

44. Airport lurker

45. Sinus MD

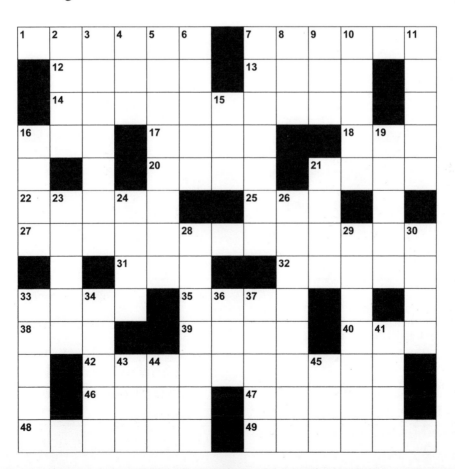

Answers on page 191.

Biblical Prophets

ACROSS

1. 23-Across, 35-Across, 51-Across, 10-Down, and 22-Down
7. Bistro name starter, often
11. Express disapproval
12. Agcy. with forest firefighters
14. Flamenco exclamation
15. Sent with Joshua to spy out the land of Canaan
17. Like religious beliefs of some Founding Fathers
19. Rain clouds
21. Tangle up
22. _____zag
23. Prophesied "the valley which was full of bones" (37:1)
25. Essayist Ralph Waldo
27. "Que _____?"
28. "CSI" find
30. Points in math class
33. Swedish university city
35. Hid a hundred prophets of God in two caves (1 Kings 18:4)
38. Word of exhortation
39. Of marriageable age
41. Some car payments
43. Monogram unit
45. Amplify
47. One in the ABA
48. Hot season for a Parisian
49. Important sports org.
50. MD's workplace
51. He openly questioned God's work

DOWN

1. Material for some pipes
2. Is accommodating
3. Metrical composition
4. "Calvin and _____"
5. Not yet settled, briefly
6. Like sports cars
8. Traveler's stopover
9. Connecticut collegians
10. Book of _____, which mentioned four chariots with differently colored horses
13. Downsized version

16. Jungian concept
18. Is suspicious
20. Big name in casual shirts
22. One of the Twelve Minor 1-Across
24. Boredom
26. Poor player
29. Pit follower
31. Rowboat device

32. _____ act
34. Irrational aversion
35. Last write-ups, for short
36. Be caught in _____
37. One of the Four Horsemen
40. Toward
42. Pointer's word
44. Green expanse
46. Map abbr.

Answers on page 191.

New Testament Prayers

ACROSS

1. Social prohibition (var.)
5. Boston's Bobby
7. Beckett's homeland
10. Eats soup loudly
12. NFL broadcaster
13. Tax collector for the ancient Romans who smote upon his breast (Luke 18:13)
15. Spanish welcome
17. Texting initials
18. Enclosure
19. Athlete Phillips
20. Bolt feature
21. Chocolate necessity
24. Burst open
28. Makes calm
30. Fatalities
31. Simple wheelless vehicle
33. Acting MacDowell
34. Cookout glowers
36. Treaty
38. Famed soprano Te Kanawa
39. First three non-consonants
42. That's-ask link
43. He begs Jesus to have mercy on him and to restore his sight (Mark 10:46–52)
45. Hollywood's Skye
46. Departure
47. French silk center
48. Atlantic st.
49. Toward

DOWN

1. Cookbook amts.
2. College grad.
3. Brothers, slangily
4. Browser bookmark
5. Coveted statuette
6. Freshened
7. 36-Down prayed that they would be filled with the knowledge of God's will
8. M-ity divider?
9. Ex-senator Bayh
11. Small flute
14. Ripened, say
16. Cantonese nut (var.)

20. What the thief on the cross prayed for (Luke 23:39–43)
21. Minn. winter hrs
22. On _____ basis
23. Clandestine org.
25. Bodily rejuvenation sought by the 43-Across, leper and paralytic
26. Not irreg.
27. Chin attachment
29. Where those in need of 25-Down are lying

32. Flowerpot filler
35. Disney mermaid
36. Prisoner who experienced an earthquake after his prayer (Acts 16:26–33)
37. Commercial award
39. Word often found at the end of the discourse with God
40. All-Star side
41. Far starters?
44. R&B's _____ Hill

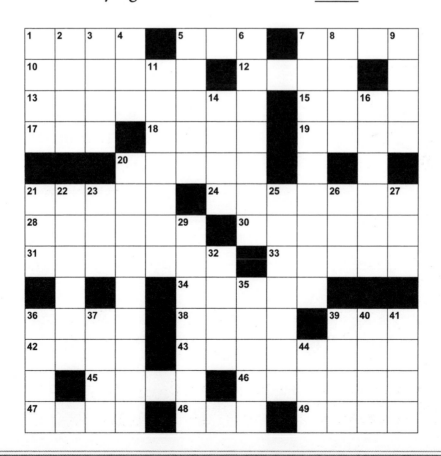

Answers on page 191.

More Words of Jesus

ACROSS

1. Went blonde, perhaps
5. Metric wts.
8. Cont. with vuvuzelas
10. "I say unto you, Love _____, bless them that curse you" (Matthew 5:44)
12. Power _____
13. Director Peter
14. California city
15. Really steamed
17. Jesus, to Mary
19. Over there, poetically
20. "With men this is impossible; but with God all _____ are possible" (Matthew 19:26)
23. Ghost
24. Stop for the "Bounty"
26. Landlocked African nation
28. Bisecting line
29. Conforming to
31. Capital of Utah, briefly
33. Pkg. for eggs
34. Meteorite remains
37. Clock climber of rhyme
41. Navigator Islands, now
42. Analogy snippet
43. Jesus gives his sheep _____ (John 10:27–28)
44. No. after a no.
45. Part of OS: abbr.
46. Singer/dancer Falana

DOWN

1. Archaic auxiliary
2. Cosmonaut Gagarin
3. Brockovich of lawsuit fame
4. Bank account increaser
5. Pressing buttons
6. FBI agent, informally
7. Indian string instrument
8. Gauging the purity of
9. "I came not to call the righteous, but sinners to _____" (Luke 5:32)
11. Auction closer?
14. "He that is without sin among you, let him first _____ at her" (John 8:7)
16. Winner's award

18. Dealing with an issue
20. Solidly built
21. Friendly exchanges
22. Treat for winter birds
23. Winter mo.
25. Wheel pivot
27. Cheap saloon

30. Largest bodies of water
32. Invisible rope pullers
35. Body image?
36. Fashion designer Burch
38. Nobel Peace Center's home
39. Gas co., for one
40. Three-seater, often

Answers on page 192.

Numbers in the Bible

ACROSS

1. "He had fasted ____ days and ____ nights" (Matthew 4:2)
5. Get punished
11. Atlas stat
12. Drive-thru order
13. Veer, like a jet
14. Consumption plan
15. "Terrible" tsar
16. Cone head?
17. They went out from Mary Magdalene (Luke 8:2)
20. Filmmaker Mervyn
21. Whale Dick
24. Eternal spirit
26. Data entered
27. Art gallery sign: abbr.
30. Give birth to
32. Compass pt.
33. Figure out
35. Caroled
37. Card game
39. Romantic emoji
42. "Gather together the dispersed of Judah from the ____ of the earth" (Isaiah 11:12)
46. Wide foot size
48. Prefix with tiller
49. Low, heavy cart
50. Title of respect
51. Be follower
52. Snake's warning
53. Backpackers' stops
54. Number of people who survived the flood (Genesis 7:13, 23)

DOWN

1. Passing crazes
2. Architectural projection
3. Steward
4. Fries, slangily
5. Secluded bay
6. Desert bloomer
7. Tennille of tunes
8. Plants used in rites by the ancient Hebrews
9. Holm of "The Hobbit"

10. How the animals boarded Noah's ark

12. Prepare for visitors

18. Loop of cord

19. Alphabet string

22. Cab alternative

23. "Wherefore they are no more twain, but _____" (Matthew 19:6)

25. Scale notes

26. Kind of circle

28. Govt. cosmetics regulator

29. Beach sights

31. Exuberant cries

34. Murmur fondly

36. Former Indian PM Indira

38. Tumult

40. Outfit again

41. Cruelly criticize

43. More than merely suggest

44. UPS containers

45. Method, for short

47. Kids' song ending

Answers on page 192.

Wisdom from Proverbs

ACROSS

1. "A good name is rather to be chosen than _____" (Proverbs 22:1)
10. Defendant's answer
11. Author Levin
12. Place in quarantine
15. Tree support
17. TV promo word
18. Relating to ancient 43-Across
20. "Don't hold back!"
22. Type of dance
23. Arena for Gen. Eisenhower
24. Productive sort
26. Front of ship
27. Lacoste of tennis
28. Bow wielder of myth
30. Doesn't let go to waste
32. Blooming time
34. Mil. rank
35. "Is that _____?"
36. Ecclesiastical assembly
39. "Better is little with the fear of the Lord than great _____" (Proverbs 15:16)

42. Big bell
43. Cinque Terre locale
44. Give approval for
46. Experience
47. End-of-page abbr.
48. "Commit thy works unto the Lord, and thy thoughts shall be _____" (Proverbs 16:3)

DOWN

2. Adhesive stuff
3. "A friend loveth at _____, and a brother is born for adversity" (Proverbs 17:17)
4. Black or green cupful
5. Per-unit price
6. Approach, as for a loan
7. Commits a sin
8. Some UFOs
9. "In all thy ways _____ him, and he shall direct thy paths" (Proverbs 3:6)
12. "Whoso loveth _____ loveth knowledge" (Proverbs 12:1)
13. Great expanse

14. Kitchen finisher?
16. Offense org.
19. Redder inside
21. Light shade of brown
25. Reeves of "Speed"
26. Geometric shapes
27. Official discharge
29. Grafton's "_____ for Ricochet"
31. Excel function
33. Tiny skin opening
35. Up till now
37. Magnetic direction
38. Add-_____
40. "Spy Hard" John _____
41. Business letter abbr.
45. "How _____ look?"

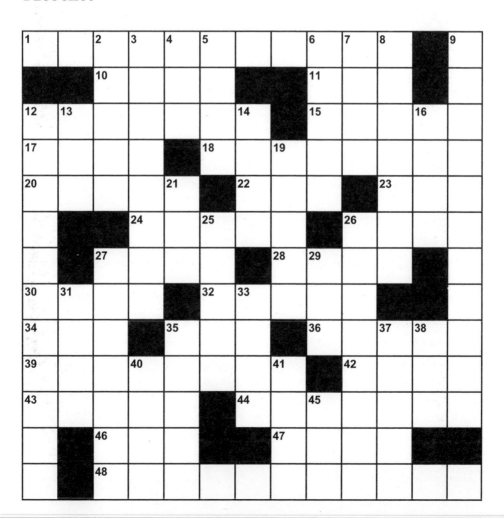

Answers on page 192.

Judges of Israel

ACROSS

1. _____ the Gileadite, an illegitimate child (Judges 11:1)
8. He killed Eglon, the king of Moab (Judges 3:21)
11. Fjord kin
12. Wickerwork willows
13. Southern shouts
14. Beach buggy, briefly
15. Regarding, on a memo
17. _____ pilot
18. Classical language
20. Kazan of film directing
21. Critiqued
24. Some drillers, for short
27. _____ the Zebulonite, buried in Aijalon (Judges 12:11)
28. Pub staple
29. Existential statement
31. What Eve was created from
32. Chem. suffix
33. Arsenal contents
36. Betting setting?
37. Hawaiian balcony
39. Impressive rating
40. White light splitter
42. On the water
45. Indian menu side
47. Screeners at JFK
48. Eyelid feature
49. Nutritious legume
50. Conversation fillers
51. The seventh of the 15, lived in Shamir (Judges 10:1)
52. Judges _____

DOWN

2. Gardner of mystery
3. Crusty desserts
4. Urges on (archaic)
5. Philly sandwich
6. Like the stars
7. Drone's home
8. Actress Alexander
9. TV channel for consumers
10. Ruby on screen
13. He was the first of the 15 (Judges 3:7–11)
16. Retrieve

19. Airborne fish-eaters
22. Empty container weight
23. Prophetess, the wife of Lapidoth, the only woman among the 15 (Judges 4:4)
25. Goose variety
26. Can be bad or good
30. The eighth of the 15, had 30 sons (Judges 10:3–5)
34. Mountain block
35. From Mogadishu
36. Less illusory
38. Sleep clinic issue
41. "Leave _____ the pros"
43. Teasdale of poetry
44. Fin ending?
45. US Open barrier
46. Excluding none

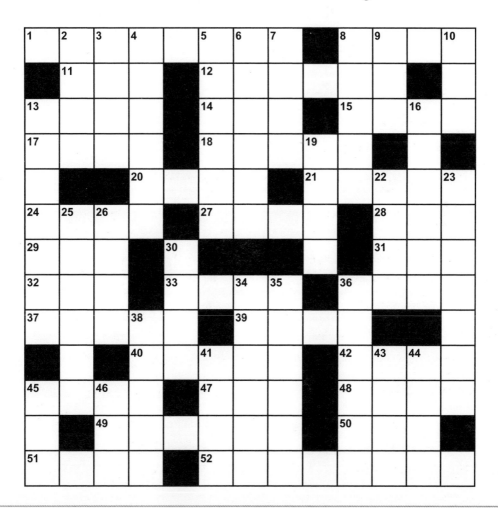

Answers on page 192.

Answers

The Prophet Daniel
(page 4)

	H	E	A	D	O	F	G	O	L	D		B
F	U	L		I	S	I		N	O	R	S	E
I	M	I	T	A	T	E		T	A	S		L
E	S	S	E		E	L	T	O	N			T
R			R	H	O	D	E		E	R	I	E
Y	E	S	N	O			D	R	E	A	M	S
F	R	A		W	H	O	S	E		N	A	H
U	N	A	B	L	E			E	R	I	C	A
R	O	B	O		A	D	D	L	E			Z
N		W	A	T	E	R		A	R	I	Z	
A		O	T	T		C	O	R	D	O	B	A
C	I	L	I	A		A	L	B		A	I	R
E		D	E	N	O	F	L	I	O	N	S	

The Sower Parable
(page 8)

	A	L	O	E		A	K	A		E	F	G
S	T	O	N	Y	P	L	A	C	E	S		O
	R	O	T	E		A	N	N	A	T	T	O
T	Y	P	O	S		S	T	E	R	O	I	D
H			O	R	K		D		P	N	G	
E		U	P	R	E	A	R		S	P	A	R
P		S	E	E	D		I	L	I	E		O
A	M	A	N		O	F	F	E	N	D		U
R	O	T		I		O	T	S				N
A	V	O	I	D	E	R		O	C	T	A	D
B	E	D	S	I	D	E		T	O	O	N	
L		A	M	O	N	G	T	H	O	R	N	S
E	L	Y		M	A	O		O	L	I	O	

The Creation Story
(page 6)

|F|A|D| |F|A|T|E| |C|A|R|D|
|O| |R|H|I|N|A|L| |O|B|I|E|
W	T	A		F	I	R	M	A	M	E	N	T
L	A	W	L	E	S	S		E	D	D	A	
	R	A	Y		T	I	N	C	T			I
E	M	B	R	Y	O		H		S	A	N	
M	A	L	E	A	N	D	F	E	M	A	L	E
I	C	E		L		A	M	E	L	I	E	
S			B	E	A	S	T		I	I	N	
S	A	T	E		C	H	A	R	N	E	L	
I	T	W	A	S	G	O	O	D		I	D	A
V	O	I	D		U	P	M	O	S	T		N
E	R	G	S		N	E	S	S		Y	T	D

"M" Names in the Bible
(page 10)

	C	L	A	M	B	E	R		M	A	R	Y
I	H	A	D		A	M	E	B	A	E		E
M	A	N	A	S	S	E	H			G	R	A	M
H			I	A	T	E			D	I	V	E
O		A	M	E	L	I	A		A	E	O	N
M	O	S	E	S		C	T	R	L		W	
E	X	I	S	T	S		S	E	E	M	E	D
	F		H	A	I	L		S	N	I	D	E
T	O	F	U		D	O	N	E	E	S		B
A	R	I	L		E	C	O	N				A
I	D	O	L		M	A	T	T	H	I	A	S
G		N	A	S	A	L	S			O	N	M	E
A	D	A	M		N	E	O	L	O	G	Y	

Answers

Name the Parable
(page 60)

CHEFS · AMERICA
REPOT · LIC · NOU
EMILE · INA · FIS
WICKEDSERVANT
E · POTSDAM · I
LISA · H · LION
MUSTARDSEED
AARP · U · TSAR
P · FIASCOS · E
PRECIOUSPEARL
OHI · SWM · ASCII
SET · LEI · SPACE
EASTERN · MYTHS

Biblical Figures
(page 64)

LOTSWIFE · SMOG
PAP · CRANIAL
NELL · OER · TEEN
I · CORNELIUS · A
C · SASSED · T · T
OUGHT · SEARCH
DALE · TOS · CORA
ELYSEE · MASON
M · C · MELTON · A
U · ELISABETH · E
SURE · HBO · HURL
MONSOON · UTA
PALO · TREASURY

Ten Commandments
(page 62)

SABBATHDAY
CANE · LAO · GOON
ONEA · ISI · ELMO
METRISTS · NONO
M · NOETIC · T
ANDEAN · SNITCH
NAILS · VENUE
DEADEN · EASTER
M · OCELLI · G
EMIR · LEONARDO
NOTA · SAP · LARD
TEED · OSE · AGES
MOUNTSINAI

Prophet Anagrams
(page 66)

UBER · JEREMIAH
SERAPE · AWOLS
DANIEL · CERISE
DBL · ERSATZ
AMA · BOURSE · E
BABEL · N · LUCK
RUE · EARLE · LAI
AIDS · I · LEAVE
H · HAGGAI · NAL
APIECE · ASP
MICRON · RHEUMY
CAPRI · GARAGE
HANANIAH · METS

Answers

Flowers & Plants
(page 68)

Biblical Nations
(page 72)

Jesus' Disciples
(page 70)

The Prophet Ezekiel
(page 74)

Answers

"M" Places in the Bible
(page 76)

Row 1: M A H A N A I M ▪ ▪ S E M ▪
Row 2: ▪ M I R E ▪ T E M P E R A
Row 3: D O R I A ▪ S H E L L A C
Row 4: ▪ R E A R M ▪ W E L S H ▪
Row 5: M O O ▪ ▪ O C U L U S ▪ P
Row 6: A S U S U A L ▪ ▪ R ▪ E
Row 7: C O T Y ▪ B A M ▪ A W O L
Row 8: E ▪ R ▪ R E P L I C A ▪
Row 9: D ▪ M I D I A N ▪ ▪ D A H
Row 10: O P I N E ▪ U D D E R ▪
Row 11: N U G G E T S ▪ I O N I C
Row 12: I N H E R I T ▪ S T E N ▪
Row 13: A S T ▪ M A K K E D A H

Bible Name Changes
(page 80)

Row 1: I B I S ▪ T W O ▪ U S P S
Row 2: T A C T ▪ H A N A N I A H
Row 3: O R E O ▪ E L O ▪ Y A D A
Row 4: O S T M A R K ▪ N O M S G ▪
Row 5: ▪ A ▪ P R E S O A K ▪
Row 6: A B Y S M S ▪ M E G A N
Row 7: M A E ▪ H A I T I ▪ O B O
Row 8: A S T R O ▪ A B I D E D
Row 9: ▪ A L K A L I S ▪ D ▪
Row 10: M A R I E ▪ B L A R I N G
Row 11: O P U S ▪ W R Y ▪ A N E W
Row 12: J E D I D I A H ▪ E D G E
Row 13: O X E N ▪ I M O ▪ L Y O N

Old Testament Prayers
(page 78)

Row 1: M I D S T ▪ H A C K J O B
Row 2: A ▪ W R I E R ▪ ▪ A R E
Row 3: R ▪ M O U N T C A R M E L
Row 4: A D O R E D ▪ C O B O L
Row 5: B O N D ▪ R E S O W ▪ Y
Row 6: O N A ▪ G I S ▪ R E G S ▪
Row 7: U N D E R S T A N D I N G
Row 8: ▪ A S W E ▪ E T S ▪ D I E
Row 9: D ▪ I B S E N ▪ S E P T
Row 10: A L I N E ▪ O S M O S E
Row 11: K I N G S O L O M O N ▪ V
Row 12: A F C ▪ P A N E L ▪ E
Row 13: R E A D A P T ▪ E T H A N

Prayers of Jesus
(page 82)

Row 1: ▪ L A Z A R U S G R A V E
Row 2: C U P ▪ T E N T ▪ L O A
Row 3: I C E H O U S E ▪ D O L T
Row 4: V ▪ M O M S ▪ A M I N E S
Row 5: I ▪ E L S E ▪ R O S S ▪ I
Row 6: C O N Y ▪ B I T C O I N
Row 7: ▪ N ▪ G N O C C H I ▪ F ▪
Row 8: R E S H A P E ▪ P H I L
Row 9: A ▪ L O D E ▪ G A L E ▪ O
Row 10: C A E S A R ▪ E L E C ▪ R
Row 11: I L E T ▪ A S S I S T E D
Row 12: N E V ▪ N O S E ▪ O N S
Row 13: E X E C U T I O N E R S ▪

Answers

Old Testament Anagrams
(page 84)

L	A	M	E	N	T	A	T	I	O	N	S	■
I	T	A	L	■			I	N	M	O	S	T
S	N	A	G	■	P	R	E	S	A	G	E	S
P	O	M	A	D	E	■	D	E	N	■	A	
E	■	R	U	T	H	■	T	I	M	O	R	
D	A	D	■	C	R	I	B	■	I	R	S	
■	D	E	U	T	E	R	O	N	O	M	Y	■
N	I	M	■	L	E	N	A	■	E	X	O	
I	M	O	F	F	■	E	Z	R	A	■	C	
H	■	R	I	C	■	E	Y	E	L	E	T	
I	N	V	A	D	E	R	S	■	G	O	R	E
L	E	A	N	E	D	■	■	I	F	I	T	
■	E	C	C	L	E	S	I	A	S	T	E	S

Bible Sayings
(page 88)

M	O	V	E	M	O	U	N	T	A	I	N	S
O	H	I	■	O	N	E	■	G	N	A	T	
A	N	A	C	O	N	D	A	■	E	S	P	Y
S	O	L	A	R	■	T	I	N	T	■		
■		G	O	L	D	E	N	C	A	L	F	
F	A	C	E	■	S	T	Y	L	E	R		
E	C	O	■	A	D	D	T	O	■	L	E	A
T	E	M	P	L	E	■	■	A	S	S	T	
A	R	M	A	G	E	D	D	O	N	■		
■	A	S	A	P	■	W	I	L	T	S		
T	E	N	S	■	S	H	E	L	L	O	U	T
A	I	D	E	■	E	A	T	■	O	N	A	
G	O	O	D	S	A	M	A	R	I	T	A	N

Name the Prophet
(page 86)

J	■	A	R	I	O	S	O	■	S	O	T	S
O	H	M	Y	■	H	A	B	A	K	K	U	K
H	■	F	E	M	A	L	E	■	I	R	M	A
N	A	M	■	A	R	A	L	■	W	A	S	T
■	I	■	L	A	D	I	D	A	■			
H	O	S	E	A	■	■	E	X	I	S	T	
O	L	A	■	C	A	L	E	B	■	S	I	P
W	I	D	T	H	■	O	R	A	L	S		
■		H	I	S	S	E	R	■	A			
A	M	E	R	■	T	E	R	A	■	E	S	S
L	O	C	O	■	U	T	A	H	A	N	■	P
B	A	R	N	A	B	A	S	■	W	I	S	E
S	N	U	G	■	S	E	E	D	E	D	■	D

King David
(page 90)

A	M	B	■	M	A	S	H	■	A	R	A	L
F	O	R	T	Y	Y	E	A	R	S	■	A	
I	T	E	■	R	E	G	R	E	T	S	■	Y
T	O	R	S	I	■	O	P	T	I	N	■	C
■		H	A	S	■	A	R	I	E	L		
D	A	V	I	D	K	I	N	G	■	V	I	A
A	V	I	A	■	Y	O	O	■	G	E	R	I
B	A	R	■	J	E	R	U	S	A	L	E	M
B	S	I	D	E	■	N	O	T	■			
L	■	L	E	T	G	O	■	W	H	I	S	K
I	■	E	L	L	I	P	S	E	■	O	U	I
N	■	F	I	V	E	S	T	O	N	E	S	
G	A	I	T	■	E	C	H	O	■	E	D	S

Answers

Fill-in-the-Blank
(page 92)

W	I	L	L	A	N	S	W	E	R		M	
	T	O	O	L	A	T	E		A	R	A	B
	O	R	B	I	T	A	L		S	A	G	E
S	O	N	S		A	T	L		H	T	M	L
A			B	L	E	S	S		T	A	I	
C	R	E	M	E		E	L	O	I	S	E	
R		D	E	S	T	I	T	U	T	E		V
I	O	D	A	T	E			G	O	R	K	I
F	L	Y		S	N	U	B	S			N	
I	D	I	G		S	L	O		G	A	N	G
C	O	N	E		I	N	S	H	O	R	E	
E	N	G	R		L	A	S	A	G	N	A	
	E		E	V	E	R	Y	W	H	E	R	E

Old Testament Prophets
(page 96)

	G	A	D		C	R	A	T	E	D		B
L	I	N	E	A	R		Z	Y	D	E	C	O
A	B	E	T		O	K	A	P	I	S		O
M	E	T	E		C	A	R	O	B			K
E			C	H	I	L	I			L	E	T	O
N	A	T	T	Y			A	R	E	A	O	F
T	R	A		M	O	T	H	S		T	M	I
A	I	R	B	N	B			V	A	S	E	S
T	A	P	A		A	G	A	P	E			A
I			T	I	D	A	L		D	R	E	I
O		B	O	N	I	T	O		I	O	T	A
N	A	R	N	I	A		H	U	L	D	A	H
S		A	S	T	H	M	A		E	S	L	

Words of Jesus
(page 94)

M	Y	F	A	T	H	E	R		T	V	G	
O		O	X	O		N	E	C		R	I	O
C	A	R	E	T		G	U	A	N	A	C	O
	L	E	D	T	O		S	A	U	C	E	D
W	I	S		E	N	T	E	N	T	E		W
O	N	E	A	R	T	H		J			O
R	E	E	D	Y		O		S	O	P	O	R
D			V		S	E	T	B	A	C	K
O		T	E	S	S	E	R	A		R	H	S
F	L	O	R	A	L		G	L	O	V	E	
G	A	M	B	L	E	S		E	V	E	R	Y
O	H	M		T	E	C		S	E	N		A
D	R	Y			T	H	E	T	R	U	T	H

Biblical Kings
(page 98)

L	A	M	E	R		A	Z	O	V			Z
E	R	Y		E	D	T		L	I	V		E
E	N	T	R	E	A	T		D	R	O	I	D
J	E	H	O	S	H	A	P	H	A	T		E
			M	E	L		A	L	E	C	K	
R	A	S	P		I	R	A	N		S	O	I
E	S	L		D	A	V	I	D		I	R	A
H	E	E		U	S	S	R		A	N	K	H
O	C	E	A	N			P	A	R			
B		K	I	N	G	S	O	L	O	M	O	N
O	P	E	R	A		A	R	I	D	I	T	Y
A		R	E	G		U	T	A		R	T	E
M		S	E	A	L			S	N	O	O	T

Answers

The Last Supper
(page 100)

Paul's Travels
(page 104)

The Persistent Widow
(page 102)

Psalm 23
(page 106)

Answers

The Prodigal Son
(page 108)

A	L	I	V	E	A	G	A	I	N			T	
	I	N	I	T	S			N	A	M	E	R	
	T	U	L	I	P		F	A	R	I	N	A	
C	U	R	E		S	P	U	N	Y	A	R	N	
O	P	E	N	S		E	N	E		M	O	S	
M		D	E	A	F	E	N		R	I	N	G	
P		S	C	A	L	E	N	E				R	
A	T	M	S		M	O	L	O	C	H		E	
S	R	A		L	I	U		T	E	A	K	S	
S	E	R	V	A	N	T	S		I	V	E	S	
I	N	C	A	S	E		M	A	V	E	N		
O	D	O	R	S			U	P	E	N	D		
N		Y	O	U	N	G	E	R	S	O	N		

The Prophetess Deborah
(page 112)

S	P	A		A	C	R	O		I	T	B	E
I	A	R	O	S	E	A	M	O	T	H	E	R
S	I	G		A	N	T	I		R	U	E	R
E	G	O	S		T	E	T	R	Y	L		O
R	E	T	I	N	A	L		I		I	S	R
A		N	A	V		S	C	H	U	S	S	
	V	I	C	T	O	R	Y	H	Y	M	N	
N	A	M	E	R	S		S	I	P			I
A	L	P		O		S	T	E	E	R	E	D
V		E	L	N	I	N	O		D	A	M	E
A	S	N	O		H	A	L	T		M	C	A
J	U	D	G	E	O	F	I	S	R	A	E	L
O	R	S	O		P	U	C	K		H	E	S

New Testament Anagrams
(page 110)

B	A	O		A	L	U	M	S		T	S	O
E	R	R		P	E	S	O	S		I	C	S
G	A	L	A	T	I	A	N	S		T	O	A
E	M	A	I	L	S		A		F	U	N	K
T	A	N	G	Y		A	R	A	L	S	E	A
S	I	D			U	N	C	L	E			
	C	O	R	I	N	T	H	I	A	N	S	
		A	N	D	E	S			E	A	T	
T	S	E	T	S	E	S		Y	O	U	V	E
A	C	T	S		R		L	E	H	M	A	N
M	A	H		E	P	H	E	S	I	A	N	S
P	R	E		G	A	U	G	E		N	N	E
A	F	L		G	Y	R	O	S		N	A	S

Joseph
(page 114)

S	A	Y	H	I		T	A	R	I	F	F	S
I	D	O		G	A	E	L		S	L	I	M
L	O	W	L	E	V	E	L		H	A	L	L
V		A	T	O	M	I	S	M		E		
E	B	A	N		C		H	E	I	D	I	
R	A	N	D		A	R	G	U	E	R		N
C	A	N	O	E	D		E	N	L	I	S	T
U		A	F	L	O	A	T		I	S	L	E
P	A	N	E	L		T		T	H	O	R	
	M		G	E	N	O	E	S	E			P
A	I	R	Y		A	R	R	E	S	T	E	R
S	N	A	P		T	B	S	P		H	I	E
H	O	S	T	E	S	S		T	O	A	S	T

Answers

Parable Anagrams
(page 116)

A	B	A	■	D	R	A	T	■	A	A	H	S
B	A	R	R	E	N	F	I	G	T	R	E	E
S	S	E	■	P	A	I	L	■	I	M	P	S
E	R	N	S	■	■	R	E	C	T	O	■	T
N	A	T	A	L	I	E	■	A	■	I	T	E
T	■	■	N	E	A	■	A	R	A	R	A	T
■	G	R	E	A	T	S	U	P	P	E	R	■
S	T	A	R	V	E	■	R	A	S	■	■	A
H	O	G	■	E	■	T	A	L	E	N	T	S
R	■	G	O	N	Z	O	■	■	S	O	W	S
E	K	E	D	■	A	N	A	T	■	T	I	E
W	E	D	D	I	N	G	G	U	E	S	T	S
D	A	Y	S	■	E	S	T	E	■	O	S	S

Workers in the Vineyard
(page 120)

■	S	H	A	L	L	B	E	F	I	R	S	T
S	E	E	M	■	S	E	G	■	■	E	U	R
■	E	L	E	V	A	T	E	■	J	A	N	E
E	S	P	R	I	T	■	S	M	U	D	G	E
Q	■	■	N	■	S	T	U	N	■	■	■	■
U	P	S	W	E	P	T	■	R	I	P	U	P
A	S	S	A	Y	■	I	■	M	O	O	S	E
L	I	A	N	A	■	E	X	U	R	B	A	N
■	■	■	T	R	E	S	■	R	■	■	■	N
N	E	V	A	D	A	■	H	E	N	L	E	Y
A	C	I	D	■	T	R	A	D	E	I	N	■
M	O	B	■	■	E	S	S	■	M	E	G	A
E	L	E	V	E	N	T	H	H	O	U	R	■

Noah's Ark
(page 118)

P	E	R	D	U	■	S	T	O	P	G	A	P
U	■	■	I	N	F	O	R	■	H	O	U	R
M	■	S	A	L	A	M	I	■	R	O	S	E
A	N	O	L	I	V	E	L	E	A	F	■	■
■	O	V	I	N	E	■	L	B	S	■	■	C
C	R	I	N	K	L	E	■	B	E	L	C	H
O	S	E	■	■	A	R	K	■	■	O	R	E
V	E	T	C	H	■	S	A	M	O	V	A	R
E	■	■	H	O	P	■	B	I	D	E	N	■
N	■	F	I	V	E	H	U	N	D	R	E	D
A	T	O	N	■	P	O	K	I	E	S	■	O
N	O	G	O	■	S	W	I	M	S	■	■	V
T	R	Y	S	A	I	L	■	S	T	O	V	E

Esther
(page 122)

H	A	D	A	S	S	A	H	■	■	P	A	T
I	C	E	U	P	■	B	I	S	M	U	T	H
D	I	T	T	O	■	U	T	T	E	R	E	R
■	D	R	O	O	P	■	I	N	L	I	N	E
A	S	A	■	F	L	O	T	S	A	M	■	E
H	■	C	A	S	E	D	■	N	■	■	■	D
A	T	T	N	■	B	O	W	■	I	A	M	A
S	■	■	T	■	R	H	E	A	S	■	■	Y
U	■	D	E	B	A	S	E	R	■	T	A	S
E	A	R	N	E	D	■	T	A	T	A	R	■
R	U	I	N	E	R	S	■	S	A	T	E	S
U	N	E	A	T	E	N	■	E	P	I	C	S
S	T	R	■	M	O	R	D	E	C	A	I	■

Answers

David's Prayers
(page 124)

Verses About Prayer
(page 128)

Mary & Martha
(page 126)

The Resurrection
(page 130)

Answers

The Good Samaritan
(page 132)

H	A	L	F	D	E	A	D		B	A	B	Y
	R	E	A		N	I	E	C	E	S		A
J	E	E	R		A	D	A		R	U	S	K
E	A	R	S		M	E	R	C	Y		P	
R			I	T	O	R		A	L	L	O	T
I	A	L		A	R	S	O	N		O	O	H
C	R	A	W	L				I	R	A	N	I
H	C	L		K	N	O	W	N		N	Y	E
O	H	A	R	E		N	O	E	L		V	
	E		A	D	I	E	U		I	L	I	E
H	O	S	T		S	I	N		S	E	A	S
O		G	E	R	U	N	D		L	A	M	
R	E	T	D		P	A	S	S	E	D	B	Y

Elijah & Elisha
(page 136)

E	L	I	J	A	H		A	L	A	N	I	S
D	A	N		L	A	P	D		D	I	N	E
D	I	S	G	O	R	G	E		U	N	I	V
Y		T	H	E	M	A	N	T	L	E		E
	B	O	A	S			O	U	T	R	U	N
E	A	R	N		W	E	I	R			T	
B	R	E	A	D	A	N	D	F	L	E	S	H
B			E	G	G	S		L	A	O	S	
T	O	O	T	L	E			A	A	R	P	
I		W	H	I	R	L	W	I	N	D		I
D	I	N	O		E	Y	E	S	O	R	E	S
E	V	E	N		R	E	E	L		U	M	A
S	E	D	G	E	S		P	E	R	M	I	T

"J" Names in the Bible
(page 134)

J	O	S	S		A	R	N		F	A	C	T
E	R	T	E		N	E	S		A	N	O	N
R	I	O	T		I	S	C	A	R	I	O	T
E	S	P	O	U	S	E		R	I	M	E	S
M	O	O	N		W	A	G	N	E	R	
I	N	F		J	O	S	H	U	A		J
A		F	A	U	N		M	E	S	A		O
H		T	R	U	C	E	S		S	A	C	
	P	O	L	I	S	H			B	E	T	H
A	R	I	E	S		E	S	C	A	P	E	E
J	O	N	A	T	H	A	N		S	T	A	B
A	S	K	S		I	P	O		R	I	S	E
M	Y	S	T		J	O	B		A	C	E	D

A Prayer of Repentance
(page 138)

	I	N	I	Q	U	I	T	I	E	S	
A	M	O	N		N	C	O		N	O	I	R
C	O	G	S		D	I	R		A	L	A	I
K	N	O	T	T	I	E	R		C	O	N	G
N		U	N	R	E	S	T			H
O	C	T	A	N	E		S	P	O	I	L	T
W	H	E	R	E			A	R	R	A	S
L	I	T	M	U	S		H	Y	S	S	O	P
E		O	P	A	Q	U	E			I
D	E	E	R		M	U	R	D	E	R	E	R
G	E	R	I		O	E	R		L	O	R	I
E	L	I	A		S	E	A		L	A	S	T
	C	L	E	A	N	H	E	A	R	T	

Answers

Biblical Mountains
(page 140)

Bible Animals
(page 144)

Isaiah
(page 142)

The Unforgiving Servant
(page 146)

Answers

Walking on Water
(page 148)

```
L O O P E R ■ M A G S ■
O ■ B E N O T A F R A I D
R E T R I M ■ G R A I N ■
D ■ U P D A T E ■ B A K U
S O S ■ N A O M I ■ ■ P
A L E X A ■ P L A C E B O
V I S ■ G R I D S ■ D O N
E N T E R O N ■ K N E L T
M ■ ■ L O U T S ■ N O H
E G A D ■ G O P A S T ■ E
■ A L E P H ■ R E H A B S
I T I S A S P I R I T ■ E
■ E A T S ■ T O P E K A
```

Bible Prophecies
(page 152)

```
R E S U R R E C T I O N ■
U M A ■ A M O ■ S K I S
N I L ■ A V O N ■ M A G I
E L A I N E ■ G O S P E L
■ I M M A N U E L ■ I L E
V O I P ■ S N E E R ■ N
I ■ S E Z ■ C ■ G E T ■ C
N ■ ■ L E D U P ■ D E L E
E S T ■ B E T R A Y A L ■
G E A R U P ■ I C E C A P
A R I E ■ O B O E ■ A N T
R I G A ■ S T R ■ K O A
F A L S E W I T N E S S
```

Paul the Apostle
(page 150)

```
D E M I ■ E P I S T L E S
A S I N I N E ■ H O P E
M P E G ■ E L M ■ A V O N
A ■ N E A R T O ■ W E S T
S ■ A P O S T L E ■
C A P R I ■ T E D E U M
U H F ■ C A B O T ■ E P I
S A C H E M ■ T O W N S
■ U S U R P E R ■ S
F L A G ■ C H U R C H ■ I
L O N G ■ K O R ■ H A L O
A C N E ■ D E N I Z E N
P H A R I S E E ■ D Y E S
```

Jesus Heals a Blind Beggar
(page 154)

```
B E G G A R ■ M A S A L A
A B O Y ■ U R I ■ A C E Y
C B E R ■ M I D ■ L A W N
K ■ S O N O F D A V I D ■
A ■ O R E L ■ A
C H E S T ■ E L D E R S
H A V E M E R C Y O N M E
E L E V E N ■ C R O S S
■ E ■ S A F E ■ S
■ B A R T I M A E U S ■ I
P E L E ■ L E I ■ N I N O
H E A L ■ E N T ■ I T O N
O B E Y E D ■ H A T E R S
```

Answers

More Psalms
(page 156)

C	L	A	P	Y	O	U	R	H	A	N	D	S
O	A	F	█	O	C	R	█	G	█	N	█	
B	L	A	C	K	T	I	E	█	H	E	A	P
B	A	R	R	E	█	A	X	I	A	L	█	A
█	█	A	L	L	H	I	S	S	I	N	S	
D	I	O	N	█	█	L	O	T	T	O	S	
O	S	U	█	P	A	T	E	N	█	E	R	A
L	A	T	H	E	S	█	█	I	S	M	S	
M	Y	F	O	R	T	R	E	S	S	█	█	
A	█	I	N	U	R	E	█	T	I	T	H	E
N	O	T	S	█	A	L	I	E	N	E	E	S
█	H	█	H	█	I	N	N	█	A	R	P	
T	H	O	U	G	H	T	S	O	F	M	A	N

Biblical Prophets
(page 160)

P	R	O	P	H	E	T	S	█	C	H	E	Z
V	█	B	O	O	█	B	L	M	█	O	L	E
C	A	L	E	B	█	D	E	I	S	T	I	C
█	N	I	M	B	I	█	E	N	M	E	S	H
Z	I	G	█	E	Z	E	K	I	E	L	█	A
E	M	E	R	S	O	N	█	█	L	█	█	R
P	A	S	A	█	D	N	A	█	L	O	C	I
H	█	█	B	█	█	U	P	P	S	A	L	A
A	█	O	B	A	D	I	A	H	█	R	A	H
N	U	B	I	L	E	█	T	O	L	L	S	
I	N	I	T	I	A	L	█	B	O	O	S	T
A	T	T	█	E	T	E	█	I	O	C	█	P
H	O	S	P	█	H	A	B	A	K	K	U	K

Ten Talents
(page 158)

L	L	A	M	A	S	█	B	A	L	E	R	S
█	E	V	E	N	T	█	E	V	I	L	█	L
█	G	A	I	N	E	D	F	I	V	E	█	O
N	O	I	█	I	L	S	A	█	█	N	E	T
O	█	L	█	S	E	L	L	█	O	A	T	H
A	D	E	P	T	█	█	L	I	D	█	H	
H	I	D	L	O	R	D	S	M	O	N	E	Y
█	G	█	U	N	O	█	█	P	R	O	L	E
O	I	L	S	█	U	G	L	I	█	S	█	L
N	N	E	█	█	G	O	I	N	█	T	I	L
T	█	E	X	C	H	A	N	G	E	R	S	
O	█	D	E	A	L	█	G	E	N	I	E	
█	P	A	S	S	B	Y	█	O	S	T	L	E	R

New Testament Prayers
(page 162)

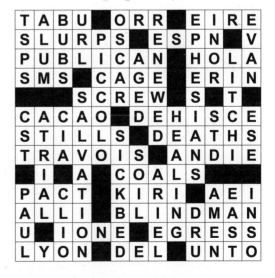

T	A	B	U	█	O	R	R	█	E	I	R	E
S	L	U	R	P	S	█	E	S	P	N	█	V
P	U	B	L	I	C	A	N	█	H	O	L	A
S	M	S	█	C	A	G	E	█	E	R	I	N
█	█	█	S	C	R	E	W	S	█	S	█	T
C	A	C	A	O	█	D	E	H	I	S	C	E
S	T	I	L	L	S	█	D	E	A	T	H	S
T	R	A	V	O	I	S	█	A	N	D	I	E
█	I	█	A	█	C	O	A	L	S	█	█	
P	A	C	T	█	K	I	R	I	█	A	E	I
A	L	L	I	█	B	L	I	N	D	M	A	N
U	█	I	O	N	E	█	E	G	R	E	S	S
L	Y	O	N	█	D	E	L	█	U	N	T	O

Answers

More Words of Jesus
(page 164)

	D	Y	E	D		K	G	S		A	F	R
Y	O	U	R	E	N	E	M	I	E	S		E
	T	R	I	P		Y	A	T	E	S		P
C	H	I	N	O		I	N	A	R	A	G	E
A			S	O	N		R		Y	O	N	
S		T	H	I	N	G	S		J	I	L	T
T	A	H	I	T	I		U	G	A	N	D	A
A	X	I	S		T	O	E	I	N	G		N
S	L	C		M		C	T	N				C
T	E	K	T	I	T	E		M	O	U	S	E
O		S	A	M	O	A		I	S	T	O	
N		E	T	E	R	N	A	L	L	I	F	E
E	X	T		S	Y	S		L	O	L	A	

Wisdom from Proverbs
(page 168)

G	R	E	A	T	R	I	C	H	E	S		A
		P	L	E	A		I	R	A		C
I	S	O	L	A	T	E		T	R	U	N	K
N	E	X	T		E	T	R	U	S	C	A	N
S	A	Y	I	T		T	A	P		E	T	O
T		M	A	K	E	R		P	R	O	W	
R	R	E	N	E		E	R	O	S		L	
U	S	E	S		A	P	R	I	L		E
C	O	L		A	N	O		S	Y	N	O	D
T	R	E	A	S	U	R	E		G	O	N	G
I	T	A	L	Y		E	N	D	O	R	S	E
O		S	E	E		C	O	N	T			
N		E	S	T	A	B	L	I	S	H	E	D

Numbers in the Bible
(page 166)

F	O	R	T	Y		C	A	T	C	H	I	T
A	R	E	A		T	O	G	O		Y	A	W
D	I	E	T		I	V	A	N		S	N	O
S	E	V	E	N	D	E	V	I	L	S		B
	L	E	R	O	Y		E		M	O	B	Y
O			S	O	U	L		I	N	P	U	T
N	F	S		S	P	A	W	N		S	S	W
E	D	U	C	E		S	A	N	G			O
F	A	R	O		B		H	E	A	R	T	
L		F	O	U	R	C	O	R	N	E	R	S
E	E	E		R	O	T	O		D	R	A	Y
S	I	R		G	I	N	S		H	I	S	S
H	O	S	T	E	L	S		E	I	G	H	T

Judges of Israel
(page 170)

J	E	P	H	T	H	A	H		E	H	U	D
	R	I	A		O	S	I	E	R	S		E
O	L	E	S		A	T	V		I	N	R	E
T	E	S	T		G	R	E	E	K		E	
H		E	L	I	A		R	A	T	E	D	
N	C	O	S		E	L	O	N		A	L	E
I	A	M		J		S			R	I	B	
E	N	E		A	R	M	S		R	E	N	O
L	A	N	A	I		A	O	N	E			R
	D		P	R	I	S	M		A	S	E	A
N	A	A	N		T	S	A		L	A	S	H
E		L	E	N	T	I	L		E	R	S	
T	O	L	A		O	F	I	S	R	A	E	L

192